MW01592803

Beowulf Simplified

Includes Modern Translation, Study Guide, Historical Context, Biography, and Character Index

BookCaps™ Study Guides

www.bookcaps.com

Beowulf

In Plain and Simple English

BookCaps Study Guides

www.bookcaps.com

Table of Contents

Error! Not a valid heading level range.

About This Series

The "Classic Retold" series started as a way of telling classics for the modern reader—being careful to preserve the themes and integrity of the original. Whether you want to understand Shakespeare a little more or are trying to get a better grasps of the Greek classics, there is a book waiting for you!

The series is expanding every month. Visit BookCaps.com to see all the books in the series, and while you are there join the Facebook page, so you are first to know when a new book comes out.

Plot

The warrior kings of Denmark began with Scyld, and after several generations his descendant, Hrothgar, came to rule. He was a just king and gathered builders from all over the world to build a great hall called Heorot. At Heorot, the people of Denmark came to drink and tell tales, and there was a time of peace. However, Grendel, a cursed descendant of Cain who lived in the swamp near Heorot became angry at their merrymaking. One night he entered the great hall and slaughtered thirty men. From then on, he terrorized Heorot and the surrounding countryside. He was so strong that no one could beat him, and tales began to spread of his strength and terror.

After over a decade, the tales spread to the land of Geat, where the great warrior hero Beowulf heard of them. Wanting to help Hrothgar and prove his worth, Beowulf set out with fourteen warriors to slay Grendel. Hrothgar is pleased but warns Beowulf that many men have tried to kill Grendel before and failed. Beowulf is so confident, however, that the Danes begin to believe in him.

That night Beowulf and his men camp in the great hall. Grendel approaches and is joyous to find warriors for him to kill. He eats one of Beowulf's men before the warrior, who was pretending to be asleep, grabbed Grendel's arm. A great fight ensues, and eventually Beowulf rips the shoulder and arm off. Realizing he is going to die, Grendel flees to the swamp, leaving his arm behind. Hrothgar is overjoyed at Beowulf's victory, and rewards him with treasure. They celebrate late into the night and fall asleep in the hall, unaware that the danger is not over.

Grendel's mother, also a strong and powerful demon, wants revenge. She enters the hall and kills one of Hrothgar's close friends, carrying his body back to her lair. Hrothgar once again asks Beowulf for help, and he agrees to go after her. They travel to the swamp and Beowulf begins to swim down to the depths. It takes him all day, but eventually he finds Grendel's mother and defeats her as well. He is given more treasure and sails back to Geatland victorious.

Eventually Beowulf becomes King when his kinsmen die, and reigns for fifty years. The time of peace ends when a thief accidentally steals a piece of treasure from a dragon underground. The dragon begins ravaging the countryside, and Beowulf realizes he must fight one more time. He chooses warriors to accompany him, and makes a great shield to defend against the dragon's fire. The dragon is about to overpower him when a young warrior named Wiglaf steps in and helps defeat the beast. Before the dragon dies, however, it bites Beowulf in the neck.

Realizing that he is about to die, Beowulf asks Wiglaf to bring him proof of the dragon's treasure. Wiglaf goes down and sees the immense pile of gold and jewels, bringing an armful back up to where Beowulf is resting. After seeing the treasure, Beowulf dies in peace. After Beowulf dies, Wiglaf is ashamed at the other warriors for being too cowardly to help during the battle.

Messages are sent throughout Geatland, and the people worry that without Beowulf to protect them war is imminent. The hero's body is burned at a funeral pyre and then buried, along with vast amounts of treasure and armor, in a barrow. His people viewed him as one of the greatest kings, and made sure that his name would never be forgotten.

Historical Context

Beowulf is an epic poem detailing the heroic acts of the Anglo-Saxon warrior king, Beowulf. Originally, it was a legends told by the Geats in Scandinavia. Like most legends and myths, Beowulf's stories were passed down orally. The poems were most likely memorized and performed by traveling storytellers who made a living by going to different cities and towns to entertain the Geatish citizens. The legend of Beowulf is compared by scholars to the Iliad and Odyssey, the epic poems which shaped Greek literature.

While the legends were passed down through the generations through oral storytelling, the poem we have today is one written long after the legend of Beowulf was originally told. Historians believe that the poem originated at around 500 A.D. and was penned some two or three hundred years later, around 700 or 800 A.D. This disparity of time is clearly marked by the migration of the Anglo-Saxons to England, where the culture began to change.

In old Scandinavia, the societal structure was based on the middle ages warrior culture in which a strong king protected his people. Like many people in the feudal ages, the Geats had a pagan religion whose roots show through very clearly in Beowulf. Many historical figures who lived around the sixth century are also present in the poem, making it easy to guess when the stories originated.

The only known manuscript of the epic, however, was penned after the migration of the Geats to England. The most obvious clue to this conclusion is the fact that the anonymous narrator of Beowulf is Christian. It was only after the migration to England that the culture began to shift away from paganism and many people converted to Christianity. The Christian influences in the copy of Beowulf we read today were most likely not in the original stories, but rather added in order to merge the old culture with the new religion. The poem itself is written in old English, a very ancient form of Germanic English brought over from Scandinavia. While it is called old English, it is virtually unrecognizable by modern day English speakers.

Beowulf was not always a famous poem - in fact, it remained in relative obscurity and was almost burned in a fire during the 18th century. It was not until the 19th century that the epic was rediscovered, and new interest was brought to it. In the early 1900's, J.R.R. Tolkien, a British author and scholar, wrote a paper on Beowulf that caused the academic world to take the poem more seriously. Today, Beowulf is largely considered an original of English literature. It is taught in high schools and colleges all over the world, although in an easy to read translation of the original old English.

Beowulf - Original and Modern Version of Text

Prelude to the Founder of the Danish House

LO, praise of the prowess of people-kings
HERE, praise the abilities of the kings of the people

of spear-armed Danes, in days long sped,
of the Danish men armed with spears, long ago

we have heard, and what honor the athelings won!
we have heard, and what honor those warriors won!

Oft Scyld the Scefing from squadroned foes,
Often, Scyld the Scefing, surrounded by enemies

from many a tribe, the mead-bench tore,
from many different tribes, he broke the peace

awing the earls. Since erst he lay
frightening the nobles. Since he was once

friendless, a foundling, fate repaid him:
friendless, an orphan, fate repaid him:

for he waxed under welkin, in wealth he throve
for he grew powerful under the sky, becoming rich

till before him the folk, both far and near
until the people both far and near

who house by the whale-path, heard his mandate
who live by the sea, came under his rule

gave him gifts: a good king he!
gave him gifts: a great king he was!

To him an heir was afterward born
Later his heir was born

a son in his halls, whom heaven sent
a son in his place, sent by heaven

to favor the folk, feeling their woe
to help out the people, feeling their sorrow

that erst they had lacked an earl for a leader
that previously they had no one to lead them

so long a while; the Lord endowed him
for such a long time; God blessed him

the Wielder of Wonder, with world's renown.
the one holding wonderful abilities, with the world's admiration and fame.

Famed was this Beowulf: far flew the boast of him,
This Beowulf [a different one from the one this poem is mostly about] was famous: his reputation was widely known

Son of Scyld, in the Scandian lands.
Son of Scyld, throughout what there was then of Scandinavia - eventually Denmark, Norway, Sweden, Finland, and Iceland.

So becomes it a youth to quit him well
So it is a good thing for a young man to make something of himself

with his father's friends, by fee and gift,
with his father's friends, through money and gifts

that to aid him, aged, in after days
in order for them to come to help him when he is old, years later

come warriors willing, should war draw nigh
soldiers will willingly help him if war comes near

liegemen loyal: by lauded deeds

loyal knights: it is by admired actions

shall an earl have honor in every clan.
shall a nobleman be honored by every community.

Forth he fared at the fated moment
Off he went at the time fate decreed

sturdy Scyld to the shelter of God.
Scyld died and his soul went to God.

Then they bore him to the ocean's billow,
Then they carried him to the ocean waves,

loving clansmen, as late he charged them,
loving family, as he had asked them to earlier,

while wielded words the winsome Scyld,
while the lovable Scyld could still talk,

the leader beloved who long had ruled...
the beloved leader who had ruled for a long time...

In the roadstead rocked a ring-dight vessel,
In the current rocked a ring-decked boat,

ice-flecked, outbound, atheling's barge:
lightly covered with ice, traveling away, a warrior's barge:

there laid they down their darling lord
there they laid down their darling lord

on the breast of the boat, the breaker-of-rings,
on the wide part of the boat, the man who had rewarded them well

by the mast the mighty one. Many a treasure,
by the mast they laid that mighty man. Many treasures,

fetched from far were freighted with him
taken from far away were in the boat with him.

No ship have I known so nobly dight
No other ship to my knowledge was so nobly decked

with weapons of war and weeds of battle,
with weapons of war and clothing of battle,

with breastplate and blade: on his bosom lay
with breastplate and sword: on his chest lay

a heaped hoard that hence should go
a piled hoard that afterwards would go

far o'er the flood with him floating away.
far over the flood with him floating away.

No less these loaded the lordly gifts,
Those who loaded the lordly gifts were of equal rank,

thanes' huge treasure, than those had done
these treasures of aristocracy, they were equal to those

who in former times forth had sent him
who in previous times had sent him out

sole on the seas, a suckling child.
all alone on the sea, as a baby.

High o'er his head they hoist the standard,
High over his head they raise the flag,

a gold-wove banner; let billows take him,
a golden banner; let the waves take him,

gave him to ocean. Grave were their spirits,
they gave him to the ocean. Their spirits were sad,

mournful their mood. No man is able
their mood was mournful. No man is able

to say in sooth, no son of the halls
to prophesy, no one born in a palace

no hero 'neath heaven - who harbored that freight!
no hero beneath heaven - who eventually took in and sheltered that ship!

~*~

Section I

Now Beowulf bode in the burg of the Scyldings,

Now Beowulf lived in the city of Scyld's followers

Leader beloved, and long he ruled

A beloved leader, and long he ruled

in fame with all folk, since his father had gone

famous to all people, since his father died

away from the world, till awoke an heir

and left the world, until his heir was born

haughty Healfdene, who held through life,

(prideful Healfdene, who continued throughout all his life,)

sage and sturdy, the Scyldings glad.

wise and healthy, which the people of Scyld were glad of.

Then, one after one, there woke to him,

Then, one after another, there was born to his family,

to the chieftain of clansmen, children four.

to Healfdene, that ruler of a tribe, four children.

Heorogar, then Hrothgar, then Halga brave;

Heorogar, then Hrothgar, then brave Halga

and I heard that --- was ---'s queen,

and I heard that so-and-so was so-and-so's queen

The Heathoscylfing's helpmate dear.

The dear spouse of the descendant of Scylf and Healfdene.

To Hrothgar was given such glory of war,

Hrothgar was fortunate in earning glory in war,

such honor of combat, that all his kin,

such honor in combat, that all his family

obeyed him gladly till great grew his band

obeyed him gladly until his followers became many

of youthful comrades. It came in his mind

young friends and allies. It came in his mind

to bid his henchmen a hall uprear,

to order his men to build a palace,

a master mead-house, mightier far

a great feasting place, far mightier

than ever was seen by the sons of earth,
than any humans had ever seen before,

and within it, then, to old and young
and inside it, then, to both old and young

he would all allot that the Lord had sent him,
he would share everything God had sent him,

save only the land and the lives of his men.
except for the land and the lives of his men.

Wide, I heard, was the work commanded,
I heard the work he ordered was vast in scope,

for many a tribe this mid-earth round,
for many tribes around this location,

to fashion the folkstead. It fell, as he ordered,
to build the great hall. It was completed, as he ordered,

in rapid achievement that ready it stood there,
in quick progress it soon was finished,

of halls the noblest: Heorot he named it
the most noble of halls: he named it Heorot [meaning "The Stag"]

whose message had might in many a land.
whose message had power in many lands.

Not reckless of promise, the rings he dealt,
Never making reckless promises, the rings he distributed [as rewards],

treasure at banquet: there towered the hall,
treasure at banquet: there was a towering hall,

high, gabled wide, the hot surge waiting
high, with wide windows, with a roaring

of furious flame. Nor far was that day
fire at the end of it. However, the day was not far

when father and son-in-law stood in feud
when father and son-in-law became enemies

for warfare and hatred that woke again.
for warfare and hatred that rose again.

With envy and anger an evil spirit
With envy and anger an evil spirit

endured the dole in his dark abode,
endured his exile in his dark home,

that he heard each day the din of revel
that he heard every day the loud festivities

high in the hall: there harps rang out,
high in the hall: there harps rang out,

clear song of the singer. He sang who knew
clear song of the singer, who knew all the

tales of the early time of man,
tales of the beginning of the world [the stories of Genesis in the Bible]

how the Almighty made the earth,
how Almighty God made the earth,

fairest fields enfolded by water,
beautiful fields covered by water,

set, triumphant, sun and moon
placed, gladly, the sun and moon

for a light to lighten the land-dwellers,
for a light to illuminate those that lived on land,

and braided bright the breast of earth
and covered the surface of the earth

with limbs and leaves, made life for all
with tree branches and leaves, made life for all

of mortal beings that breathe and move.
of living things that breath and move.

So lived the clansmen in cheer and revel
So lived the people in cheerful happiness

a winsome life, till one began
a lovely life, until one began

to fashion evils, that field of hell.
to create and do evil, that specialty of hell.

Grendel this monster grim was called,
This grim monster was called "Grendel",

march-riever mighty, in moorland living,
a powerful invading monster, living in the swamp,

in fen and fastness; fief of the giants
in wild land and isolation; home of the giants

the hapless wight a while had kept
the unfortunate creature a while had stayed

since the Creator his exile doomed.
since God doomed him to exile.

On kin of Cain was the killing avenged
The family of Cain [the first murderer, son of Adam] were punished for the killing

by sovran God for slaughtered Abel.
by vengeful God for the murdered Abel [Cain's brother].

Ill fared his feud, and far was he driven,
His fight was doomed, and he was driven far,

for the slaughter's sake, from sight of men.
for the sake of his murder, he was sent away from the rest of humanity.

Of Cain awoke all that woeful breed,
From Cain descended all those awful beings,

Etins and elves and evil-spirits,
Devils and elves [in those days considered bad] and evil spirits,

as well as the giants that warred with God
As well as the giants that fought against God

weary while: but their wage was paid them!
for a long time: but they received what they deserved!!

~*~

16

Section II

WENT he forth to find at fall of night

[Grendel] went forth at nightfall to find

that haughty house, and heed wherever

that proud palace, and pay attention to wherever

the Ring-Danes, outrevelled, to rest had gone.

the Ring-Danes, having celebrated to exhaustion, had gone to rest.

Found within it the atheling band

Found inside it the group of warriors

asleep after feasting and fearless of sorrow

asleep after feasting and without any fears

of human hardship. Unhallowed wight.

of human hardship. Unholy monster,

grim and greedy, he grasped betimes

grim and greedy, he went and hunted

wrathful, reckless, from resting-place,

angry, reckless, from his home,

thirty of the thanes, and thence he rushed

thirty of the warriors, and from there he rushed

fain of his fell spoil, faring homeward

away from his prey, heading home

laden with slaughter, his lair to seek

covered with blood, seeking his lair

Then at the dawning, as day was breaking,

Then at dawn, as day was breaking,

'

the might of Grendel to men was known

men came to know the power of Grendel

then after wassail was wail uplifted

then after the ceremony they uplifted a cry of sorrow

loud moan in the morn. The mighty chief

loud weeping in the morning. The mighty chief

atheling excellent, unblithe sat

an excellent warrior, unhappily sat

labored in woe for the loss of his thanes

filled with sorrow for the loss of his men

when once had been traced the trail of the fiend

when once the path of the villain had been traced

spirit accurst: too cruel that sorrow

a cursed spirit: that sorrow was too cruel

too long, too loathsome. Not late the respite

too long, too loathsome. The break was not long,

with night returning, anew began

when night returned, it began again

ruthless murder; he recked no whit

ruthless murder; he had no notion

firm in his guilt, of the feud and crime.

firmly guilty, of the fight and crime.

They were easy to find who elsewhere sought

Those who looked elsewhere were easy to find

in room remote their rest at night,

in their faraway rooms where they slept,

bed in the bowers, when that bale was shown

bed in the outer cottages, when that bale was shown

was seen in sooth, with surest token, --

was seen in a vision, with the definite sign, --

the hall-thane's hate. Such held themselves

the ruler of the hall's hate. These men moved themselves

far and fast who the fiend outran

far and fast, who outran the fiend

Thus ruled unrighteous and raged his fill

And in this way he ruled unrighteously and raged all he [Grendel] wished

one against all; until empty stood

one against all; until it was empty

that lordly building, and long it bode so

that noble building, and it continued so for a long time

Twelve years' tide the trouble he bore,

He [the king] bore twelve years' tide of trouble

sovran of Scyldings, sorrows in plenty

leader of Scyldings, filled with sorrow

boundless cares. There came unhidden

and unlimited worries. There came out of hiding

tidings true to the tribes of men,

true tales to the other tribes of people,

in sorrowful songs, how ceaselessly Grendel

in sad songs, how Grendel endlessly

harassed Hrothgar, what hate he bore him

harassed Hrothgar, what hatred he had for him

what murder and massacre, many a year,

what murder and massacres, for many years,

feud unfading, -- refused consent

his fighting never fading, -- he refused to agree

to deal with any of Daneland's earls,

to deal with any Danish nobles,

make pact of peace, or compound for gold

to make a truce, or stop fighting in exchange for money

still less did the wise men ween to get

still less did wise men attempt to get

great fee from the feud from his fiendish hands

any large profit from the fighting from this villain.

But the evil one ambushed old and young
But the evil one [Grendel] ambushed both old and young

death-shadow dark, and dogged them still,
dark as the shadow of death, and followed closely after them still,

lured, or lurked in the livelong night
lured, or lurked in the long-lived night

of misty moorlands: men may say not
of misty moorlands: man may not say

where the haunts of these Hell-Runes be.
where the customary places of these monsters are.

Such heaping of horrors the hater of men,
Such ongoing horrors the hater of men,

lonely roamer, wrought unceasing,
lonely roamer, made without stopping,

harassings heavy. O'er Heorot he lorded,
harrassing them constantly. He dominated Heorot,

gold-bright hall, in gloomy nights;
that bright and golden palace, in gloomy nights;

and ne'er could the prince approach his throne,
and the prince could never approach his throne,

-- 'twas judgment of God, -- or have joy in his hall.
-- it was the judgment of God -- or enjoy his own palace.

Sore was the sorrow to Scyldings'-friend,
The sadness of that ally of the people once ruled by Scyld was intense,

heart-rending misery. Many nobles
heartbreaking misery. Many nobles

sat assembled, and searched out counsel
sat together, and looked for advice

how it were best for bold-hearted men
on what would be the best way for brave men

against harassing terror to try their hand.
to fight back against this harassing terror.

Whiles they vowed in their heathen fanes
While they promised in their non-Christian manner

altar-offerings, asked with words
animal sacrifices, prayed with words

that the slayer-of-souls would succor give them
that the killer would give them mercy

for the pain of their people. Their practice this,
from the pain of their people. Their religious customs,

their heathen hope; 'twas Hell they thought of
their non-Christian hopes; it was Hell they thought of

in mood of their mind. Almighty they knew not,
in their mood at the time. They did not know God,

Doomsman of Deeds and dreadful Lord,
The powerful and stern Christian God,

nor Heaven's-Helmet heeded they ever,
nor had they listened to the words of His son,

Wielder-of-Wonder. -- Woe for that man
the Miracle Worker [Jesus Christ]. -- There will be doom for that man,

who in harm and hatred hales his soul
who when suffering and full of hate tries to recover his soul

to fiery embraces; -- nor favor nor change
in deals with other spirits; -- no good fortune or change

awaits he ever. But well for him
can he wait for. But it is good for the man

that after death-day may draw to his Lord,
that after dying may come nearer to his God,

and friendship find in the Father's arms!
and find friendship in his [Heavenly] Father's arms!

~*~

Section III

THUS seethed unceasing the son of Healfdene
IN THIS WAY the son of Healfdene worried constantly

with the woe of these days; not wisest men
with the suffering of this time; not even the wisest men

assuaged his sorrow; too sore the anguish,
could lessen his sadness; the anguish was too intense,

loathly and long, that lay on his folk,
awful and long, that his people were feeling,

most baneful of burdens and bales of the night.
the worst of burdens and reasons to fear the night.

This heard in his home Hygelac's thane,
One of Hygelac's men heard of this,

great among Geats, of Grendel's doings.
a great man among the Geats, he heard of Grendel's actions.

He was the mightiest man of valor
He was the most courageous and capable man

in that same day of this our life,
in that same period of life as ours,

stalwart and stately. A stout wave-walker
steadfast and stately. A well-made ship

he bade make ready. Yon battle-king, said he,
he ordered to be prepared. This battle-king, he said,

far o'er the swan-road he fain would seek,
far over the sea he chose to seek out,

the noble monarch who needed men!
the royal ruler who needed men!

The prince's journey by prudent folk
Sensible people felt that the prince's journey

was little blamed, though they loved him dear;
had little to criticize, though they loved him very much;

they whetted the hero, and hailed good omens.
they gave the hero provisions and wished him good luck.

And now the bold one from bands of Geats
And now the brave one, from the Geats people,

comrades chose, the keenest of warriors
chose men to go with him, the most eager of warriors

e'er he could find; with fourteen men
he could ever find; with fourteen men

the sea-wood he sought, and, sailor proved,
he looked for a ship, and, once they had one,

led them on to the land's confines.
led them away to the border of their country.

Time had now flown; afloat was the ship,
Time had passed; the ship was afloat,

boat under bluff. On board they climbed,
a boat under a cliff. They climbed on board,

warriors ready; waves were churning
the warriors were ready; waves were churning

sea with sand; the sailors bore
the water together with the sand; the sailors wore,

on the breast of the bark their bright array,
as they stood in the front of the ship, their bright clothing,

their mail and weapons: the men pushed off,
their chain-mail and weapons: the men pushed off,

on its willing way, the well-braced craft.
without any resistance, that well-reinforced ship.

Then moved o'er the waters by might of the wind
Then they moved over the waters by the power of the wind

that bark like a bird with breast of foam,
that cries like a bird with a breast of foam,

till in season due, on the second day
until in due time, on the second day

the curved prow such course had run
the curved prow of the ship had run such a course

that sailors now could see the land,
that the sailors could now see the land,

sea-cliffs shining, steep high hills,
shining sea cliffs; high, steep hills,

headlands broad. Their haven was found,

broad headlands. They had found their destination,

their journey ended. Up then quickly
their journey had ended. Up then quickly

the Weders' clansmen climbed ashore,
the Weders' [another name for this tribe] clansmen climbed ashore,

anchored their sea-wood, with armor clashing
anchored their ship, with their armor clashing

and gear of battle: God they thanked
and all their battle gear: they thanked God

for passing in peace o'er the paths of the sea.
for their peaceful passage over the paths of the sea.

Now saw from the cliff a Scylding clansman,
Now one of the people of Scyld saw them,

a warden that watched the water-side,
a guard that guarded the shore,

how they bore o'er the gangway glittering shields,
how they carried over the gangway glittering shields,

war-gear in readiness; wonder seized him
their war-gear all ready; curiosity grabbed him

to know what manner of men they were.
to know what kind of men they were.

Straight to the strand his steed he rode,
He rode his horse straight to the strand,

Hrothgar's henchman; with hand of might
Hrothgar's henchman; with a mighty hand

he shook his spear, and spake in parley.
he shook his spear, and spoke in diplomacy.

"Who are ye, then, ye armed men,
"Who are you then, you armed men,

mailed folk, that yon mighty vessel
people wearing chainmail, that this mighty vessel

have urged thus over the ocean ways,
have sailed in this way over the ocean,

here o'er the waters? A warden I,
here over the waters? I am a warden,

sentinel set o'er the sea-march here,
a guard set over the sea-march here,

lest any foe to the folk of Danes
in case any enemy to the Danish people

with harrying fleet should harm the land.
with a fleet of warships should harm the land.

No aliens ever at ease thus bore them,
No foreigners ever so comfortably carried them,

linden-wielders: yet word-of-leave
clothes and weapons such as yours: yet permission

clearly ye lack from clansmen here,
you clearly lack from the people here,

my folk's agreement. -- A greater ne'er saw I
my folk's agreement. -- I never saw a greater

of warriors in world than is one of you, -
warrior in this world than just one of you, -

yon hero in harness! No henchman he
hero in harness over there! He is no henchman

worthied by weapons, if witness his features,
made more impressive by weapons, as told by his appearance,

his peerless presence! I pray you, though, tell
his presence without equal! I beg you, though, tell

your folk and home, lest hence ye fare
me where you come from, so that you do not afterwards become

suspect to wander your way as spies
suspected as spies, wandering your way

in Danish land. Now, dwellers afar,
in Denmark. Now, you men from far away,

ocean-travellers, take from me
travellers on the ocean, take from me

simple advice: the sooner the better
simple advice: it would be better the sooner

I hear of the country whence ye came."
I hear of the country from where you came."

~*~

To him the stateliest spake in answer;
The stateliest of the men answered him;

the warriors' leader his word-hoard unlocked: --
the warriors' leader unleased his eloquence: --

"We are by kin of the clan of Geats,
"We belong to the clan of Geats,

and Hygelac's own hearth-fellows we.
and we are family to Hygelac.

To folk afar was my father known,
My father was known even far away,

noble atheling, Ecgtheow named.
he was a noble warrior named Ecgtheow.

Full of winters, he fared away
Old in years, he passed away

aged from earth; he is honored still
died of his age; he is still honored

through width of the world by wise men all.
far and wide by all wise men.

To thy lord and liege in loyal mood
To your lord and ruler in a loyal mood

we hasten hither, to Healfdene's son,
we are hurrying to meet Healfdene's son,

people-protector: be pleased to advise us!
protector of the people: please give us advice!

To that mighty-one come we on mickle errand,
To that mighty one we come on a quest,

to the lord of the Danes; nor deem I right
to the lord of the Danes; I do not think it right

that aught be hidden. We hear -- thou knowest
for this to be a secret. We hear - you know

if sooth it is -- the saying of men,
if it is true -- men say,

that amid the Scyldings a scathing monster,
that among the Scyldings a viscious monster,

dark ill-doer, in dusky nights
doer of dark deeds, in dark nights

shows terrific his rage unmatched,
shows terrible rage without equal,

hatred and murder. To Hrothgar I
hatred and murther. I will bring to Hrothgar

in greatness of soul would succor bring,
in my generosity, relief,

so the Wise-and-Brave may worst his foes, --
so the king may overcome his enemies, --

if ever the end of ills is fated,
if the end of troubles is ever to come,

of cruel contest, if cure shall follow,
the cure for cruel conflict,

and the boiling care-waves cooler grow;
and the boiling waves of worries grow cooler;

else ever afterward anguish-days
or else forever times of anguish

he shall suffer in sorrow while stands in place
he shall suffer while still in place

high on its hill that house unpeered!"
that unmatched palace stands on the hill!"

Astride his steed, the strand-ward answered

Atop his horse, the guard of the strand answered

clansman unquailing: "The keen-souled thane

the unafraid clansman: "The eager ruler

must be skilled to sever and sunder duly

must be skilled to end and duly separate

words and works, if he well intends.

words and deeds, if he has good intentions.

I gather, this band is graciously bent

I gather, this group is well meaning

to the Scyldings' master. March, then, bearing

towards the leader of the Scyldings. March then, carrying

weapons and weeds the way I show you.

weapons and supplies in the direction I show you.

I will bid my men your boat meanwhile

I will tell my men to meanwhile

to guard for fear lest foemen come, --

to guard your boat in case enemies come, --

your new-tarred ship by shore of ocean

your newly built ship by the ocean shore

faithfully watching till once again

faithfully watching, until once again

it waft o'er the waters those well-loved thanes

it transports over the waters those well-loved nobles

-- winding-neck'd wood, -- to Weders' bounds,

-- winding-necked wood, -- to the borders of the Weder lands,

heroes such as the hest of fate

such heroes that at the hand of fate

shall succor and save from the shock of war."

shall be spared and saved from the shock of war."

They bent them to march, -- the boat lay still,

They began to march, -- the boat lay still,

fettered by cable and fast at anchor

chained down by cables and solidly anchored

broad-bosomed ship. -- Then shone the boars

broad and wide ship. -- Then shone the pictures of wild boars

over the cheek-guard; chased with gold

over the cheek-guards of their helmets; decorated with gold

keen and gleaming, guard it kept

bright and gleaming, it kept guard

o'er the man of war, as marched along

over the man of war [the ship], as marched along

heroes in haste, till the hall they saw,

the heroes hastily, till they saw the hall,

broad of gable and bright with gold:

with broad gables, bright with gold:

that was the fairest, 'mid folk of earth,

that was the most beautiful, among the people of earth,

of houses 'neath heaven, where Hrothgar lived,

of houses beneath heaven, where Hrothgar lived,

and the gleam of it lightened o'er lands afar.

and the gleam of it brought light over lands far and wide.

The sturdy shieldsman showed that bright

The sturdy shield-carrying warrior showed that bright

burg-of-the-boldest; bade them go

city of the courageous; called upon them to go

straightway thither; his steed then turned,

there straightaway; then turning his steed,

hardy hero, and hailed them thus: --

great hero, and gave them this goodbye:--

"'Tis time that I fare from you. Father Almighty

"It is time that I leave you. Almighty God

in grace and mercy guard you well,

may he in grace and mercy guard you well,

safe in your seekings. Seaward I go

safe in your search. I go back towards the sea

'gainst hostile warriors hold my watch."

to watch out for hostile warriors.

~*~

Section V

STONE-BRIGHT the street: it showed the way
THE STREET of bright stones showed the way

to the crowd of clansmen. Corselets glistened
to the crowd of clansmen. Bracelets glistened

hand-forged, hard; on their harness bright
hand-forged, hard; bright on their harness

the steel ring sang, as they strode along
the steel ring banged harmoniously, as they walked along

in mail of battle, and marched to the hall.
in battle chain mail, and marched to the hall.

There, weary of ocean, the wall along
There, tired of the ocean, along the wall

they set their bucklers, their broad shields, down,
they set down their equipment and broad shields,

and bowed them to bench: the breastplates clanged,
and sat to rest: there breastplates clanged,

war-gear of men; their weapons stacked,
men's war gear; their weapons stacked,

spears of the seafarers stood together,
spears of the sea travellers stood together,

gray-tipped ash: that iron band
gray-tipped ash [wood] : that sturdy and brave band

was worthily weaponed! -- A warrior proud
was worthily weaponed! -- A proud warrior

asked of the heroes their home and kin.
asked the heroes where they came from.

"Whence, now, bear ye burnished shields,
"From where, now, you carry polished shields,

harness gray and helmets grim,
gray harness and impressive helmets,

spears in multitude? Messenger, I,
and many spears? I am a messenger,

Hrothgar's herald! Heroes so many
Hrothgar's official spokesman! So many heroes -

ne'er met I as strangers of mood so strong.
I have never met strangers so strong and brave looking.

'Tis plain that for prowess, not plunged into exile,
It's obvious that it's because of your ability, not because of exile,

for high-hearted valor, Hrothgar ye seek!"
for your great courage, that you are meeting Hrothgar!"

Him the sturdy-in-war bespake with words,
He our hero spoke with words,

proud earl of the Weders answer made,
proud nobleman of the Weders replied,

hardy 'neath helmet: -- "Hygelac's, we,
heardy beneath his helmet: "We are Hygelac's men,

fellows at board; I am Beowulf named.
allies; I am named Beowulf.

I am seeking to say to the son of Healfdene
I intend to say to the son of Healfdene

this mission of mine, to thy master-lord,
this mission of mine, to your leader,

the doughty prince, if he deign at all
that enduring prince, if he generously allows at all

grace that we greet him, the good one, now."
permission that we greet him, the good one, now."

Wulfgar spake, the Wendles' chieftain,
Wulfgar spoke, who was the Wendles' chief,

whose might of mind to many was known,
whose great intelligence was known to many,

his courage and counsel: "The king of Danes,
his courage and wisdom. "The king of Danes,

the Scyldings' friend, I fain will tell,
the Scyldings' friend, I surely will tell,

the Breaker-of-Rings, as the boon thou askest,
the Breaker-of-Rings, of the request you made,

the famed prince, of thy faring hither,
the famed prince, of you arriving here,

and, swiftly after, such answer bring
and, quickly afterward, bring back whatever answer

as the doughty monarch may deign to give."
the enduring king may generously choose to give."

Hied then in haste to where Hrothgar sat
They quickly went to where Hrothgar sat

white-haired and old, his earls about him,
white-haired and old, his nobles all around him,

till the stout thane stood at the shoulder there
until the reliable thane approached the side

of the Danish king: good courtier he!
of the Danish king: a good courtier he was!

Wulfgar spake to his winsome lord: --
Wulfgar spoke to his lovable lord: --

"Hither have fared to thee far-come men
"Here have traveled to you men from far away

o'er the paths of ocean, people of Geatland;
over the currents of the ocean, people of Geatland;

and the stateliest there by his sturdy band
and the most dignified, standing with his sturdy band of soldiers,

is Beowulf named. This boon they seek,
is named Beowulf. The request they make,

that they, my master, may with thee
that they, sir, might with you

have speech at will: nor spurn their prayer
speak freely: do not turn down their desire

to give them hearing, gracious Hrothgar!
for you to listen, gracious Hrothgar!

In weeds of the warrior worthy they,
In clothes of worthy warriors,

methinks, of our liking; their leader most surely,
in my opinion, the sort we like; their leader definitely

a hero that hither his henchmen has led."
is a hero that has led his henchmen here.

~*~

Section VI

HROTHGAR answered, helmet of Scyldings: --

HROTHGAR, the leader of Scyldings, answered: --

"I knew him of yore in his youthful days;

"I knew him long ago when he was young;

his aged father was Ecgtheow named,

his old father was named Ecgtheow,

to whom, at home, gave Hrethel the Geat

who gave Hrethel the Geat

his only daughter. Their offspring bold

his only daughter. Their children bold

fares hither to seek the steadfast friend.

comes here to look for the loyal friend.

And seamen, too, have said me this, --

And sailors, too, have told me this, --

who carried my gifts to the Geatish court

the ones who carried my gifts to the royal court of the Geats

thither for thanks, -- he has thirty men's

there for thanks, -- he has thirty men's

heft of grasp in the gripe of his hand,

strength in his grasp,

the bold-in-battle. Blessed God

Beowulf the brave in battle. Blessed God

out of his mercy this man hath sent

out of his mercy has sent this man

to Danes of the West, as I ween indeed,

to Danes of the West, as I believe indeed,

against horror of Grendel. I hope to give

against the horror of Grendel. I hope to give

the good youth gold for his gallant thought.

the good youth payment for his gallant idea.

Be thou in haste, and bid them hither,

Hurry, and tell them to come to me,

clan of kinsmen, to come before me

clan of kinsmen, to come stand in front of me

and add this word, -- they are welcome guests

and add this message, -- they are welcome guests

to folk of the Danes."

to the Danish people."

[To the door of the hall

[To the door of the hall

Wulfgar went] and the word declared: --

Wulfgar went] and announced: --

"To you this message my master sends,

"My master sends this message to you:

East-Danes' king, that your kin he knows,

king of the East Danes says he knows your people,

hardy heroes, and hails you all

as hardy heroes, and greets you all joyously

welcome hither o'er waves of the sea!

with welcome here over the waves of the sea!

Ye may wend your way in war-attire

You may walk around in war clothing and armor

and under helmets Hrothgar greet;

and greet Hrothgar with your helmets on;

but let here the battle-shields bide your parley

but let the battle-shields wait out your meeting here

and wooden war-shafts wait its end."

and your wooden spears also wait for you to finish the conference."

Uprose the mighty one, ringed with his men,

Up stood the mighty one, encircled by his men,

brave band of thanes: some bode without,

that brave band of thanes: some stayed outside,

battle-gear guarding, as bade the chief.

guarding the battle gear, as Beowulf told them.

Then hied that troop where the herald led them,

Then the troop went where the herald led them,

under Heorot's roof: [the hero strode,]

under Heorot's roof: [the hero strode,]

hardy 'neath helm, till the hearth he neared.

hardy beneath his helmet, until he neared the hearth.

Beowulf spake, -- his breastplate gleamed,

Beowulf spoke, -- his breastplate gleamed,

war-net woven by wit of the smith: --

chain mail for war woven by the skill of the smith: --

"Thou Hrothgar, hail! Hygelac's I,

"You, Hrothgar, hello! I am Hygelac's man,

kinsman and follower. Fame a plenty

kinsman and follower. Much fame

have I gained in youth! These Grendel-deeds

I have gained when young! These actions of Grendel

I heard in my home-land heralded clear.

I heard in my homeland the news clearly delivered.

Seafarers say how stands this hall,

Sea travelers say how this hall stands,

of buildings best, for your band of thanes

best of buildings, for your band of thanes,

empty and idle, when evening sun

empty and unused, while the evening sun

in the harbor of heaven is hidden away.

is hidden away in the depths of the sky.

So my vassals advised me well, --

So my courtiers advised me well, --

brave and wise, the best of men, --

brave and wise, they are the best of men, --

O sovran Hrothgar, to seek thee here,

Oh sovereign Hrothgar, to seek you here,

for my nerve and my might they knew full well.

for my bravery and ability they knew full well.

Themselves had seen me from slaughter come

They have seen me come from slaughter

blood-flecked from foes, where five I bound,

covered in blood from enemies, where I destroyed five,

and that wild brood worsted. I' the waves I slew

and defeated that wild brood. In the waves I killed

nicors by night, in need and peril

water demons by night, in danger and duty

avenging the Weders, whose woe they sought, --

avenging the Weders, whose suffering they sought, --

crushing the grim ones. Grendel now,

crushing the grim ones. Grendel now,

monster cruel, be mine to quell

monster cruel, be mine to stop

in single battle! So, from thee,

in single battle! So, from you,

thou sovran of the Shining-Danes,

sovereign of the Shining Danes,

Scyldings'-bulwark, a boon I seek, --

leader of the Scyldings, I make a request, --

and, Friend-of-the-folk, refuse it not,

and, Friend-of-the-folk, do not refuse,

O Warriors'-shield, now I've wandered far, --

O king, now that I have come so far, --

that I alone with my liegemen here,

that I alone with my loyal men here,

this hardy band, may Heorot purge!

this hardy band, may free Heorot of this menace!

More I hear, that the monster dire,

I also here, that the terrible monster,

in his wanton mood, of weapons recks not;

in his rampages carries no weapons

hence shall I scorn -- so Hygelac stay,

so I will go without – so Hygelac stay,

king of my kindred, kind to me! –

king of my people, kind to me! –

brand or buckler to bear in the fight,

any kind of weapon to have in the fight,

gold-colored targe: but with gripe alone

or a flag to fight under: but with my bare hands

must I front the fiend and fight for life,

must I face the fiend and fight for life,

foe against foe. Then faith be his

foe against foe. Then I believe

in the doom of the Lord whom death shall take.

that God will decide who will live and die.

Fain, I ween, if the fight he win,

Indeed, I believe, if he wins the fight,

in this hall of gold my Geatish band

in this hall of gold my group of Geats

will he fearless eat, -- as oft before, --

will he fearlessly eat, -- as often before, --

my noblest thanes. Nor need'st thou then

my noblest thanes. So you will have no need

to hide my head; for his shall I be,

to bury me; for I shall be his,

dyed in gore, if death must take me;

red with blood, if death must take me;

and my blood-covered body he'll bear as prey,

and my blood-covered body he'll treat as prey,

ruthless devour it, the roamer-lonely,

devour it ruthlessly, Grendel,

with my life-blood redden his lair in the fen:

and turn his lair red with my life-blood:

no further for me need'st food prepare!

so you will not have to prepare any food for me!

To Hygelac send, if Hild should take me,

Send to Hygelac, if the goddess of death should take me,

best of war-weeds, warding my breast,

my best war clothing, that sheltered my body,

armor excellent, heirloom of Hrethel

excellent armor, that I inherited from Hrethel

and work of Wayland. Fares Wyrd as she must."

made by Wayland [the Norse god of smiths and metalwork]. The goddess of Fate does what she has to.

~*~

Section VII

HROTHGAR spake, the Scyldings'-helmet: --

HROTHGAR spoke, the leader of Scyldings:--

"For fight defensive, Friend my Beowulf,

"To defend us, Beowulf my friend,

to succor and save, thou hast sought us here.

to relieve and save us, you have sought us here.

Thy father's combat a feud enkindled

Your father's war began a feud

when Heatholaf with hand he slew

when he killed Heatholaf

among the Wylfings; his Weder kin

among the Wylfings; his Weder relatives

for horror of fighting feared to hold him.

were afraid to have him around for horror of fighting.

Fleeing, he sought our South-Dane folk,

Escaping, he sought our South-Dane folk,

over surge of ocean the Honor-Scyldings,

over the ocean waves, the Honor-Scyldings,

when first I was ruling the folk of Danes,

when I was first ruling the Danish people,

wielded, youthful, this widespread realm,

and was a young king over this widespread realm,

this hoard-hold of heroes. Heorogar was dead,

this place full of heroes. Heorogar was dead,

my elder brother, had breathed his last,

my older brother, had breathed his last,

Healfdene's bairn: he was better than I!

Healfdene's child, he was better than I!

Straightway the feud with fee I settled,

I stopped the war with bribes straight away,

to the Wylfings sent, o'er watery ridges,

sent to the Wylflings, over the watery waves,

treasures olden: oaths he swore me.

ancient treasures: he made me many promises.

Sore is my soul to say to any

Sad is my soul to say to any

of the race of man what ruth for me

of the race of man what it means to me

in Heorot Grendel with hate hath wrought,

what Grendel has done in Heorot through his hate,

what sudden harryings. Hall-folk fail me,

what sudden attacks. Hall-folk fail me,

my warriors wane; for Wyrd hath swept them

my warriors dwindle in number; for Fate has swept them

into Grendel's grasp. But God is able

into Grendel's hands. But God is able

this deadly foe from his deeds to turn!

to stop this deadly foe!

Boasted full oft, as my beer they drank,

Often they bragged, as my beer they drank,

earls o'er the ale-cup, armed men,

earls over ale, armed men,

that they would bide in the beer-hall here,

that they would respond in the beer-hall here,

Grendel's attack with terror of blades.

to Grendel's attack with their own swords.

Then was this mead-house at morning tide

Then was this mead-house by dawn

dyed with gore, when the daylight broke,

red with blood, when the daylight broke,

all the boards of the benches blood-besprinkled,

the boards of the benches all sprinkled with blood,

gory the hall: I had heroes the less,

the hall all gory: I had fewer heroes then,

doughty dear-ones that death had reft.

enduring dear ones that death had doomed.

-- But sit to the banquet, unbind thy words,

-- But sit to the banquet, talk freely,

hardy hero, as heart shall prompt thee."

hardy hero, to your heart's desire."

Gathered together, the Geatish men

Gathered together, Beowulf's men

in the banquet-hall on bench assigned,

on their assigned benches in the banquet-hall,

sturdy-spirited, sat them down,

strong of spirit, sat down,

hardy-hearted. A henchman attended,

hardy-hearted. A servant attended,

carried the carven cup in hand,

carried the carved ceremonial cup in hand,

served the clear mead. Oft minstrels sang

served the clear mead. Minstrels often sang

blithe in Heorot. Heroes revelled,

happily in Heorot. Heroes reveled,

no dearth of warriors, Weder and Dane.

there was no lack of warriors, both Weder and Dane.

~*~

Section VIII

UNFERTH spake, the son of Ecglaf,
UNFERTH, the son of Ecglaf, spoke,

who sat at the feet of the Scyldings' lord,
who sat at the feet of the Scyldings' ruler,

unbound the battle-runes. -- Beowulf's quest,
looking for a fight. -- Beowulf's quest,

sturdy seafarer's, sorely galled him;
that sturdy sailor's, intensely irritated him;

ever he envied that other men
he always envied that other men

should more achieve in middle-earth
should achieve more earthly

of fame under heaven than he himself. --
fame under heaven than he himself. --

"Art thou that Beowulf, Breca's rival,
"Are you that Beowulf, Breca's rival,

who emulous swam on the open sea,
who swam, copying him, on the open sea,

when for pride the pair of you proved the floods,
when for pride the pair of you tested the waves,

and wantonly dared in waters deep
and recklessly dared in deep waters

to risk your lives? No living man,
to risk your lives? No man living,

or lief or loath, from your labor dire
or any other considerations, from your unwise action

could you dissuade, from swimming the main.
could change your mind, from swimming the main.

Ocean-tides with your arms ye covered,
You covered ocean-tides with your arms' strokes,

with strenuous hands the sea-streets measured,
with your hands' strenuous swimming you measured the sea,

swam o'er the waters. Winter's storm
swam over the waters. Winter's storm

rolled the rough waves. In realm of sea
rolled the rough waves. In the world of the se

a sennight strove ye. In swimming he topped thee,
for five nights you tried. In swimming he outmatched you,

had more of main! Him at morning-tide
had more ability! Him at dawn

billows bore to the Battling Reamas,
the waves carried him to the Battling Reamas,

whence he hied to his home so dear
from where he travelled to his home so dear

beloved of his liegemen, to land of Brondings,
beloved of his soldiers and servants, to the land of the Brondings,

fastness fair, where his folk he ruled,
that beautiful castle, where he ruled his people,

town and treasure. In triumph o'er thee
town and treasure. In triumph over you

Beanstan's bairn, his boast achieved.
Beanstan's child, he confirmed his bragging.

So ween I for thee a worse adventure
So imagine I for you a worse adventure

-- though in buffet of battle thou brave hast been,
-- though in the struggle of battle you have been brave,

in struggle grim, -- if Grendel's approach
in grim struggle, -- if Grendel's approach

thou darst await through the watch of night!"
you dare await throughout the night!"

Beowulf spake, bairn of Ecgtheow: --
Beowulf spoke, the child of Ecgtheow: --

"What a deal hast uttered, dear my Unferth,
"You have said a lot, my dear Unferth,

drunken with beer, of Breca now,
drunk with beer, of Breca now,

told of his triumph! Truth I claim it,
told of his triumph! I claim it is true,

that I had more of might in the sea
that I had more strength in the sea

than any man else, more ocean-endurance.
than any other man, more ocean-endurance.

We twain had talked, in time of youth,
We two had talked, in our younger days,

and made our boast, -- we were merely boys,
and made our boast, -- we were only boys,

striplings still, -- to stake our lives
children still, -- to risk our lives

far at sea: and so we performed it.
far at sea: and so we did it.

Naked swords, as we swam along,
Unsheathed swords, as we swam along,

we held in hand, with hope to guard us
we held in hand, hoping they would protect us

against the whales. Not a whit from me
against the whales. Not even a small distance from me

could he float afar o'er the flood of waves,
could he float afar over the waves,

haste o'er the billows; nor him I abandoned.
speed over the billows; and I did not abandon him.

Together we twain on the tides abode
Together the two of us on the tides stayed

five nights full till the flood divided us,
for five full nights until the floor divided us,

churning waves and chillest weather,
churning waves and the chilliest weather,

darkling night, and the northern wind
darkest night, and the northern wind

ruthless rushed on us: rough was the surge.
ruthlessly rushed on us: the surge was rough.

Now the wrath of the sea-fish rose apace;
Now the anger of the sea-fish rose against us;

yet me 'gainst the monsters my mailed coat,
yet my chain-mail coat against the monsters,

hard and hand-linked, help afforded, --
hard and hand-linked, gave me help, --

battle-sark braided my breast to ward,
battle armor covered my chest,

garnished with gold. There grasped me firm
garnished with gold. There firmly grasped me

and haled me to bottom the hated foe,
and hauled me to the bottom the hated foe,

with grimmest gripe. 'Twas granted me, though,
with grimmest grim. It was granted me, though,

to pierce the monster with point of sword,
to stab the monster with the point of my sword,

with blade of battle: huge beast of the sea
with blade of battle: the huge sea creature

was whelmed by the hurly through hand of mine.
was overwhelmed on the sea floor through my hand.

~*~

Section IX

ME thus often the evil monsters
OFTEN the evil monsters threatened me

thronging threatened. With thrust of my sword,
all surrounding. With the thrust of my sword,

the darling, I dealt them due return!
the darling, I fought them back!

Nowise had they bliss from their booty then
In no way did they have the pleasure of capturing

to devour their victim, vengeful creatures,
and devouring their victim, vengeful creatures,

seated to banquet at bottom of sea;
seated to feast at the bottom of the sea;

but at break of day, by my brand sore hurt,
but at break of day, so deeply hurt by me,

on the edge of ocean up they lay,
floating on the surface of the ocean they lay,

put to sleep by the sword. And since, by them
killed by the sword. And since, by them

on the fathomless sea-ways sailor-folk
on the bottomless sea the sailor-folk

are never molested. -- Light from east,
are never attacked. -- Light from east,

came bright God's beacon; the billows sank,
came the sunrise; the waves lessened,

so that I saw the sea-cliffs high,
so that I saw the high sea cliffs,

windy walls. For Wyrd oft saveth
windy walls. For Fate often saves

earl undoomed if he doughty be!
a fortunate man if he endures!

And so it came that I killed with my sword

And so it happened that I came with my sword

nine of the nicors. Of night-fought battles
nine of the sea monsters. Of battles fought by night

ne'er heard I a harder 'neath heaven's dome,
never have I heard a harder one beneath heaven

nor adrift on the deep a more desolate man!
or a more desolate man adrift on the deep!

Yet I came unharmed from that hostile clutch,
Yet I came unharmed from that hostile meeting,

though spent with swimming. The sea upbore me,
though exhausted with swimming. The sea carried me up,

flood of the tide, on Finnish land,
flood of the tide, to Finnish land,

the welling waters. No wise of thee
the swelling waters. Never

have I heard men tell such terror of falchions,
have I heard men tell such terror of beasts,

bitter battle. Breca ne'er yet,
bitter battle. Breca never yet,

not one of you pair, in the play of war
not one of you pair, in the course of war

such daring deed has done at all
has done such a daring deed

with bloody brand, -- I boast not of it! --
with bloody weapon, -- I do not brag about it! --

though thou wast the bane of thy brethren dear,
though you were the enemy of your own dear brethren

thy closest kin, whence curse of hell
your closest relatives, from where the curse of hell

awaits thee, well as thy wit may serve!
awaits you, no matter how smart your mouth!

For I say in sooth, thou son of Ecglaf,

For I say in truth, you son of Ecglaf,

never had Grendel these grim deeds wrought,
Grendel would never have done such grim deeds,

monster dire, on thy master dear,
terrible monster, on your dear master

in Heorot such havoc, if heart of thine
in Heorot such havoc, if your heart

were as battle-bold as thy boast is loud!
were as brave as your proud talk is loud!

But he has found no feud will happen;
But he has found there will be no fight;

from sword-clash dread of your Danish clan
from the fierce swords of your Danish clan

he vaunts him safe, from the Victor-Scyldings.
he considers himself save from the Scyldings.

He forces pledges, favors none
He gets his own way, respects none

of the land of Danes, but lustily murders,
of the land of the Danes, but eagerly murders

fights and feasts, nor feud he dreads
fights and feasts, nor opposition he fears

from Spear-Dane men. But speedily now
from Danish fighters. But speedily now

shall I prove him the prowess and pride of the Geats,
I shall show him the prowess and pride of the Geats,

shall bid him battle. Blithe to mead
shall call him to battle. Cheerfully to mead

go he that listeth, when light of dawn
goes he that listens, when the light of dawn

this morrow morning o'er men of earth,
tomorrow morning over men of earth,

ether-robed sun from the south shall beam!"

the early sun from the south shall beam!

Joyous then was the Jewel-giver,
The Jewel-giver was filled with joy,

hoar-haired, war-brave; help awaited
thick-haired, brave in war; help awaited

the Bright-Danes' prince, from Beowulf hearing,
the Bright-Dane's prince, from what he heard from Beowulf,

folk's good shepherd, such firm resolve.
the good leader of the people, such firm resolve.

Then was laughter of liegemen loud resounding
The men laughed loud and hearty

with winsome words. Came Wealhtheow forth,
with winning words. Wealhtheow came forth,

queen of Hrothgar, heedful of courtesy,
queen of Hrothgar, keeping courtesy in mind,

gold-decked, greeting the guests in hall;
gold-decked, greeting the hall's guests;

and the high-born lady handed the cup
and the aristocratic lady handed the cup

first to the East-Danes' heir and warden,
first to the East-Dane's heir and leader,

bade him be blithe at the beer-carouse,
asked him to be cheerful at the beer party,

the land's beloved one. Lustily took he
the land's beloved one. He eagerly took

banquet and beaker, battle-famed king.
the food and drink, that king famous in battle.

Through the hall then went the Helmings' Lady,
The queen then went through the hall

to younger and older everywhere
to everyone everywhere

carried the cup, till come the moment
carried the cup, until the moment came

when the ring-graced queen, the royal-hearted,
when the jewel-covered queen, the royal-hearted

to Beowulf bore the beaker of mead.
took the beaker of mead to Beowulf.

She greeted the Geats' lord, God she thanked,
She greeted the Geats' lord, thanking God

in wisdom's words, that her will was granted,
in wise words, that her wish was granted,

that at last on a hero her hope could lean
that at last she had a hero to pin her hopes to

for comfort in terrors. The cup he took,
for comfort in terrors. He took the cup,

hardy-in-war, from Wealhtheow's hand,
strong-in-war, from Wealtheow's hand

and answer uttered the eager-for-combat.
and the eager-for-combat answered.

Beowulf spake, bairn of Ecgtheow: --
Beowulf spoke, the son of Ecgtheow: --

"This was my thought, when my thanes and I
"This was my thought, when my men and I

bent to the ocean and entered our boat,
traveled to the ocean and entered our boat,

that I would work the will of your people
that I would fulfill your people's wishes

fully, or fighting fall in death,
fully, or die fighting for them,

in fiend's gripe fast. I am firm to do
in the fiend's fast grip. I am resolved to do

an earl's brave deed, or end the days
a nobleman's brave deed, or end the days

of this life of mine in the mead-hall here."
of this life of mine in this mead-hall."

Well these words to the woman seemed,
These words impressed the woman,

Beowulf's battle-boast. -- Bright with gold
Beowulf's battle-boast. -- Bright and golden

the stately dame by her spouse sat down.
the stately lady sat down by her spouse.

Again, as erst, began in hall
Again, as before, began in the hall

warriors' wassail and words of power,
warriors' cheering and powerful words,

the proud-band's revel, till presently
the celebration of the proud band, until eventually

the son of Healfdene hastened to seek
the son of Healfdene hurried to get

rest for the night; he knew there waited
rest for the night; he knew there would be

fight for the fiend in that festal hall,
a fight against the fiend in that festive hall,

when the sheen of the sun they saw no more,
when the sunshine had finally gone,

and dusk of night sank darkling nigh,
and dusk of night sank darkly near,

and shadowy shapes came striding on,
and shadowy shapes came striding in,

wan under welkin. The warriors rose.
pale under the sky. The warriors rose.

Man to man, he made harangue,
Man to man, he gave greetings,

Hrothgar to Beowulf, bade him hail,
Hrothgar to Beowful, wished him luck,

let him wield the wine hall: a word he added: --
let him use the wine hall: he added a few words: --

"Never to any man erst I trusted,
"Never to a man before I have trusted,

since I could heave up hand and shield,
since I could pick up a shield,

this noble Dane-Hall, till now to thee.
this noble Dane-Hall, until to you now.

Have now and hold this house unpeered;
Have now and take care of this matchless house;

remember thy glory; thy might declare;
remember your glory; your strength declare;

watch for the foe! No wish shall fail thee
watch for the foe! Your ability will not fail you

if thou bidest the battle with bold-won life."
if you go through the battle with bold-won life."

~*~

Section X

THEN Hrothgar went with his hero-train,
THEN Hrothgar went with his attendants,

defence-of-Scyldings, forth from hall;
defence-of-Scyldings, away from the hall;

fain would the war-lord Wealhtheow seek,
the warlord would look for Wealhtheow,

couch of his queen. The King-of-Glory
couch of his queen. The glorious king

against this Grendel a guard had set,
had set a guard against Grendel,

so heroes heard, a hall-defender,
so the heroes heard, a defender of the hall,

who warded the monarch and watched for the monster.
who protected the monarch and watched for the monster.

In truth, the Geats' prince gladly trusted
In truth, the Geats' prince trusted completely

his mettle, his might, the mercy of God!
his courage, his strenght, and the mercy of God!

Cast off then his corselet of iron,
Cast of then his iron armor,

helmet from head; to his henchman gave, --
his helmet from his head; he gave to his henchman, --

choicest of weapons, -- the well-chased sword,
the best of weapons, -- the well-made sword,

bidding him guard the gear of battle.
telling him to guard the battle gear.

Spake then his Vaunt the valiant man,
The valiant man spoke then,

Beowulf Geat, ere the bed be sought: --
Beowulf the Geat, before they went to bed: --

"Of force in fight no feebler I count me,

"Of my force in fight, I consider myself no feebler

in grim war-deeds, than Grendel deems him.
in grim war-deeds, than Grendel thinks himself.

Not with the sword, then, to sleep of death
I will not kill him with a sword, then

his life will I give, though it lie in my power.
though it lies in my power.

No skill is his to strike against me,
It takes no skill for him to strike against me,

my shield to hew though he hardy be,
to break my shield however strong he is,

bold in battle; we both, this night,
bold in battle: both of us, tonight,

shall spurn the sword, if he seek me here,
shall not use the sword, if he seeks me here,

unweaponed, for war. Let wisest God,
without weapons, for war. Let wisest God,

sacred Lord, on which side soever
sacred Lord, choose the side

doom decree as he deemeth right."
to be doomed as he considers it right."

Reclined then the chieftain, and cheek-pillows held
The chieftain then lay down, and pillows held

the head of the earl, while all about him
the head of the earl, while all around him

seamen hardy on hall-beds sank.
the hardy sailors lay on hall beds.

None of them thought that thence their steps
Not of them thought that from there their steps

to the folk and fastness that fostered them,
to their families and homes that they came from,

to the land they loved, would lead them back!

would lead them back to the land they loved!

Full well they wist that on warriors many
Full well they knew that many warriors

battle-death seized, in the banquet-hall,
died in battle, in that banquet-hall

of Danish clan. But comfort and help,
of the Danes. But comfort and help,

war-weal weaving, to Weder folk
healing their war worries, to Weder folk,

the Master gave, that, by might of one,
the Master gave, that, by the power of one,

over their enemy all prevailed,
over their enemy all would survive and win,

by single strength. In sooth 'tis told
by single strength. In wisdom it is told

that highest God o'er human kind
that highest God over humanity

hath wielded ever! -- Thro' wan night striding,
has always ruled over! -- Through the dark night striding,

came the walker-in-shadow. Warriors slept
came the walker-in-shadow [Grendel]. Warriors slept

whose hest was to guard the gabled hall, --
whose job was to guard the gabled hall, --

all save one. 'Twas widely known
all but one. It was widely known

that against God's will the ghostly ravager
that against God's will the ghostly ravager

him could not hurl to haunts of darkness;
he could not hurl to haunts of darkness;

wakeful, ready, with warrior's wrath,
wakeful, ready, with the anger of a warrior,

bold he bided the battle's issue.
bold he waited for the beginning of battle.

~*~

XI

THEN from the moorland, by misty crags,
THEN from the moor, by misty cliffs,

with God's wrath laden, Grendel came.
with God's anger upon him, Grendel came.
The monster was minded of mankind now
The monster was thinking of the humans now

sundry to seize in the stately house.
various ones to devour in the stately house.

Under welkin he walked, till the wine-palace there,
Under the sky he walked, until the wine-palace there,

gold-hall of men, he gladly discerned,
the golden hall of men, he gladly saw,

flashing with fretwork. Not first time, this,
flashing with ornate decoration. This was not the first time,

that he the home of Hrothgar sought, --
that he went to the home of Hrothgar, --

yet ne'er in his life-day, late or early,
yet never in his life, late or early,

such hardy heroes, such hall-thanes, found!
did he find such hardy heroes and soldiers!

To the house the warrior walked apace,
The warrior walked a while to the house,

parted from peace; the portal opended,
parted from peace; opened the gate,

though with forged bolts fast, when his fists had struck it,
though it was bolted shut, when his fists had hit it,

and baleful he burst in his blatant rage,
and bad-tempered he burst in his obvious rage,

the house's mouth. All hastily, then,
the house's door. All hastily, then,

o'er fair-paved floor the fiend trod on,
over the beautifully paved floor the fiend stepped on,

ireful he strode; there streamed from his eyes
full of anger he strode; there streamed from his eyes

fearful flashes, like flame to see.
frightening flashes, like flame to see.

He spied in hall the hero-band,
He noticed in the hall the hero-band,

kin and clansmen clustered asleep,
kin and clansmen asleep all together,

hardy liegemen. Then laughed his heart;
hardy liegemen. He laughed inside;

for the monster was minded, ere morn should dawn,
for the monster planned, before the morning dawned,

savage, to sever the soul of each,
savagely, to rip the soul from each,

life from body, since lusty banquet
life from from body, since an eager feast

waited his will! But Wyrd forbade him
waited for him! But Fate forbade him

to seize any more of men on earth
to grab any more men on earth

after that evening. Eagerly watched
after that night. Eagerly watched

Hygelac's kinsman his cursed foe,
Hygelac's kinsman his destined foe,

how he would fare in fell attack.
how he would manage in an evil attack.

Not that the monster was minded to pause!
Not that the monster planned on pausing!

Straightway he seized a sleeping warrior
Straight away he seized a sleeping warrior

for the first, and tore him fiercely asunder,
for the first, and fiercely tore him apart,

the bone-frame bit, drank blood in streams,
bit his bones, drank blood in streams,

swallowed him piecemeal: swiftly thus
swallowed him bit by bit, in this way, quickly,

the lifeless corse was clear devoured,
the lifeless corpse was completely devoured,

e'en feet and hands. Then farther he hied;
even feet and hands. Then farther he moved;

for the hardy hero with hand he grasped,
he reached out for the hardy hero with a grasping hand,

felt for the foe with fiendish claw,
felt for the foe with fierce claws

for the hero reclining, -- who clutched it boldly,
for the hero lying down, -- who clutched it boldly,

prompt to answer, propped on his arm.
quick to answer, propped on his arm.

Soon then saw that shepherd-of-evil
Soon then the evil monster saw

that never he met in this middle-world,
that he had never met in this world,

in the ways of earth, another wight
in the ways of earth, another being

with heavier hand-gripe; at heart he feared,
with a stronger grip; at heart he feared,

sorrowed in soul, -- none the sooner escaped!
his soul saddened, -- and soon escaped!

Fain would he flee, his fastness seek,
He wanted to run away, find his fortress,

the den of devils: no doings now
the den of devils: no deeds now

such as oft he had done in days of old!
such as often he had done in other days!

Then bethought him the hardy Hygelac-thane
Then the hardy Hygelac-thane thought

of his boast at evening: up he bounded,
of his boast earlier that evening: up he bounded,

grasped firm his foe, whose fingers cracked.
firmly grasped his foe, whose fingers cracked.

The fiend made off, but the earl close followed.
The fiend turned and ran, but the nobleman followed closely.

The monster meant -- if he might at all --
The monster meant -- if he could at all --

to fling himself free, and far away
to get himself flung free, and far away

fly to the fens, -- knew his fingers' power
escape to the marshes -- knew his fingers' power

in the gripe of the grim one. Gruesome march
in the grip of the grim one. A gruesome path

to Heorot this monster of harm had made!
to Herot this harmful monster had made!

Din filled the room; the Danes were bereft,
Noise filled the room, the Danes had been deprived,

castle-dwellers and clansmen all,
those that lived in the castle, and their families,

earls, of their ale. Angry were both
nobles, of their ale. Angry were both

those savage hall-guards: the house resounded.
those savage guards: the house echoed with sound.

Wonder it was the wine-hall firm
It fills one with amazement that the wine-hall

in the strain of their struggle stood, to earth
in the strain of their struggle stood, on it foundation

the fair house fell not; too fast it was
the beautiful house did not collapse, too solid it was

within and without by its iron bands
inside and outside by its iron rings

craftily clamped; though there crashed from sill
skillfully clamped; though there crashed from its place

many a mead-bench -- men have told me --
many of the mead benches -- men have told me --

gay with gold, where the grim foes wrestled.
cheerful with gold, where the grim foes wrestled.

So well had weened the wisest Scyldings
So well had planned the wisest Scyldings

that not ever at all might any man
that not any amount of destruction

that bone-decked, brave house break asunder,
would cause that bone-decked, brave house would break apart,

crush by craft, -- unless clasp of fire
crushed intentionally, -- unless a fire

in smoke engulfed it. -- Again uprose
swallowed it in some. -- Again rose up

din redoubled. Danes of the North
noise redoubled. Danes of the North

with fear and frenzy were filled, each one,
were filled with fear and frenzy, every one of them,

who from the wall that wailing heard,
who heard that wailing from the wall,

God's foe sounding his grisly song,
God's foe screaming his grisly howls,

cry of the conquered, clamorous pain
cries of the conquered, loud pain

from captive of hell. Too closely held him
from captive of hell. Beowulf held him too closely,

he who of men in might was strongest
he who of men in power was strongest

in that same day of this our life.
of his era and ours.

~*~

Section XII

NOT in any wise would the earls'-defence
NOT in any way would the nobles'-defence

suffer that slaughterous stranger to live,
allow that murderous stranger to live,

useless deeming his days and years
thinking his life was useless   ꞌ

to men on earth. Now many an earl
to men on earth. Now many a noble,

of Beowulf brandished blade ancestral,
ancestors of Beowulf, brandished blades

fain the life of their lord to shield,
to protect the life of their lord,

their praised prince, if power were theirs;
their praised prince, if in their power;

never they knew, -- as they neared the foe,
they never knew, -- as they neared the foe,

hardy-hearted heroes of war,
strong-hearted heroes of war,

aiming their swords on every side
aiming their swords at every side

the accursed to kill, -- no keenest blade,
to kill the cursed monster, -- no sharpest blade,

no farest of falchions fashioned on earth,
no shiniest of swords created on earth,

could harm or hurt that hideous fiend!
could harm and hurt that ugly creature!

He was safe, by his spells, from sword of battle,
He was safe, through his magic spells, from sword fo battle,

from edge of iron. Yet his end and parting
from iron blades. Yet his end and parting

on that same day of this our life
in our era

woeful should be, and his wandering soul
should be full of trouble, and his wandering soul

far off flit to the fiends' domain.
floats far away to the fiends' domain [Hell].

Soon he found, who in former days,
Soon he found, who in earlier days,

harmful in heart and hated of God,
evil and hated of God,

on many a man such murder wrought,
murdering so many men,

that the frame of his body failed him now.
that the strength of his body failed him now.

For him the keen-souled kinsman of Hygelac
For he the eager kinsman of Hygelac [Beowulf]

held in hand; hateful alive
held in his hand; they would hate

was each to other. The outlaw dire
each other when alive. The awful outlaw

took mortal hurt; a mighty wound
took a fatal injury; a mighty wound

showed on his shoulder, and sinews cracked,
showed on his shoulder, and tendons cracked,

and the bone-frame burst. To Beowulf now
and his bones burst. To Beowful now

the glory was given, and Grendel thence
the glory was given, and Grendel from there

death-sick his den in the dark moor sought,
ran to his den in the dark moor, dying

noisome abode: he knew too well
that disgusting home: he knew too well

that here was the last of life, an end
that here was the end of his life,

of his days on earth. -- To all the Danes
the end of his days on Earth. -- To all the Danes

by that bloody battle the boon had come.
by that bloody battle the blessing had come.

From ravage had rescued the roving stranger
The roving stranger had rescued from ruin

Hrothgar's hall; the hardy and wise one
Hrothgar's hall; the enduring and wise one

had purged it anew. His night-work pleased him,
had cleansed it of vermin once more. His night's work pleased him,

his deed and its honor. To Eastern Danes
his accomplishment and its honor. To Eastern Danes

had the valiant Geat his vaunt made good,
had the valiant Geat kept his promise,

all their sorrow and ills assuaged,
all their sadness and troubles taken care of,

their bale of battle borne so long,
their curse of battle they suffered so long,

and all the dole they erst endured
and all the events they had earlier endured

pain a-plenty. -- 'Twas proof of this,
plenty of pain. -- It was proof of this,

when the hardy-in-fight a hand laid down,
when the winner of the fight put down a hand,

arm and shoulder, -- all, indeed,
arm and shoulder, -- all, indeed,

of Grendel's gripe, -- 'neath the gabled roof.
Grendel's ripped-off limb, -- beneath the gabled roof.

~*~

Section XIII

MANY at morning, as men have told me,
MANY warriors that morning, as I have been told,

warriors gathered the gift-hall round,
gathered around the gift-hall,

folk-leaders faring from far and near,
chiefs coming from far and near,

o'er wide-stretched ways, the wonder to view,
over long roads, to see the amazing sight,

trace of the traitor. Not troublous seemed
memento of the monster. It did not seem troubling

the enemy's end to any man
the enemy's death, to any man

who saw by the gait of the graceless foe
who saw by the footprints of the graceless foe

how the weary-hearted, away from thence,
how the exhausted, away from there,

baffled in battle and banned, his steps
overcome in battle and cast out, his steps

death-marked dragged to the devils' mere.
marked with death dragged to the devils' marsh.

Bloody the billows were boiling there,
The waves were churning and bloody there,

turbid the tide of tumbling waves
tremendous the tumbling tides

horribly seething, with sword-blood hot,
horribly rolling, hot with blood,

by that doomed one dyed, who in den of the moor
bled by the doomed one, who in den of the moor

laid forlorn his life adown,
died lonely and lost

his heathen soul, and hell received it.

his non-Christian soul, and hell received it.

Home then rode the hoary clansmen
The cheerful clansmen rode home then,

from that merry journey, and many a youth,
from that happy journey, and many a young man,

on horses white, the hardy warriors,
on white horses, the hardy warriors,

back from the mere. Then Beowulf's glory
back from the marsh. Then Beowulf's glory

eager they echoed, and all averred
the eagerly repeated, and all claimed

that from sea to sea, or south or north,
that all throughout the world,

there was no other in earth's domain,
there was no other on earth,

under vault of heaven, more valiant found,
under the height of heaven, more valiant to be found,

of warriors none more worthy to rule!
no warrior was more worthy to rule!

(On their lord beloved they laid no slight,
(To their beloved lord they meant no insult,

gracious Hrothgar: a good king he!)
gracious Hrothgar: a good king he was!)

From time to time, the tried-in-battle
From time to time, those experienced in battle

their gray steeds set to gallop amain,
set their horses to gallop together,

and ran a race when the road seemed fair.
and ran a race when the road seemed good.

From time to time, a thane of the king,
From time to time, a member of the king's court,

who had made many vaunts, and was mindful of verses,

who had accomplished great things, and was familiar with poetry,

stored with sagas and songs of old,
his memory full of sagas and songs of old,

bound word to word in well-knit rime,
word to word connected in clever rhyme,

welded his lay; this warrior soon
constructed his epic; this warrior soon

of Beowulf's quest right cleverly sang,
sang cleverly of Beowulf's quest,

and artfully added an excellent tale,
and skillfully added an excellent tale,

in well-ranged words, of the warlike deeds
in well-chosen words, of the warlike deeds

he had heard in saga of Sigemund.
the singer had heard in the saga of Sigemund.

Strange the story: he said it all, --
The story was amazing: he told it all, --

the Waelsing's wanderings wide, his struggles,
the Waelsing's many travels, his struggles,

which never were told to tribes of men,
which never were told to the general public,

the feuds and the frauds, save to Fitela only,
the fighting and trickery, except to Fitela,

when of these doings he deigned to speak,
when he chose to speak of these doings,

uncle to nephew; as ever the twain
uncle to nephew; since always the two

stood side by side in stress of war,
stood side by side in the chaos of war,

and multitude of the monster kind
and many, many monsters

they had felled with their swords. Of Sigemund grew,

they had killed with their swords. Of Sigemund grew,

when he passed from life, no little praise;
when he died, much praise;

for the doughty-in-combat a dragon killed
for the enduring-in-combat killed a dragon

that herded the hoard: under hoary rock
that guarded much treasure: under solid rock

the atheling dared the deed alone
the warrior dared to do the deed alone

fearful quest, nor was Fitela there.
frightening quest, nor was Fitela there.

Yet so it befell, his falchion pierced
Yet so it happened, his sword stabbed

that wondrous worm, -- on the wall it struck,
that incredible dragon, -- on the wall it struck,

best blade; the dragon died in its blood.
best blade; the dragon died bloodily.

Thus had the dread-one by daring achieved
In this way had the dread-one by daring achieved

over the ring-hoard to rule at will,
over the treasure-hoard to use as he wished,

himself to pleasure; a sea-boat he loaded,
however he pleased; a sea-boat he loaded,

and bore on its bosom the beaming gold,
and carried on it the gleaming gold,

son of Waels; the worm was consumed.
son of Waels; the dragon's body decayed.

He had of all heroes the highest renown
He had of all heroes the greatest renown

among races of men, this refuge-of-warriors,
among all of humanity, this protector of warriors,

for deeds of daring that decked his name

for deeds of daring associated with his name

since the hand and heart of Heremod
since the health and strength of Heremod

grew slack in battle. He, swiftly banished
grew weak in battle. He, swiftly exiled

to mingle with monsters at mercy of foes,
to go among monsters at the mercy of foes,

to death was betrayed; for torrents of sorrow
to death was betrayed; for many troubles

had lamed him too long; a load of care
had crippled him for too long; with a load of worries

to earls and athelings all he proved.
he was tested by nobles and warriors.

Oft indeed, in earlier days,
Often indeed, in earlier days,

for the warrior's wayfaring wise men mourned,
wise men wished he would not wander,

who had hoped of him help from harm and bale,
the ones who had hoped he'd protect them from harm and evil,

and had thought their sovran's son would thrive,
and had thought their sovereign's son would thrive,

follow his father, his folk protect,
be like his father, protect his people,

the hoard and the stronghold, heroes' land,
the hoard and the fortress, heroes' land,

home of Scyldings. -- But here, thanes said,
home of the people of Scyld. -- But here, nobles said,

the kinsman of Hygelac kinder seemed
the kinsman of Hygelac seemed kinder

to all: the other was urged to crime!
to all: the other was inclined to crime!

And afresh to the race, the fallow roads

[Back on topic] And returning to the race, the empty roads

by swift steeds measured! The morning sun
were raced over by fast horses! The morning sun

was climbing higher. Clansmen hastened
was climbing higher. Clansmen rushed

to the high-built hall, those hardy-minded,
to the hall on the hill, those hardy-minded,

the wonder to witness. Warden of treasure,
to see the sight. Guardian of treasure,

crowned with glory, the king himself,
crowned with glory, King Hrothgar,

with stately band from the bride-bower strode;
with his entourage strode from the master bedroom;

and with him the queen and her crowd of maidens
and with him the queen and her ladies in waiting

measured the path to the mead-house fair.
traveled the path to the beautiful mead-house.

~*~

Section XIV

HROTHGAR spake, -- to the hall he went,
HROTHGAR spoke, -- he went to the hall,

stood by the steps, the steep roof saw,
stood by the steps, saw the steep roof,

garnished with gold, and Grendel's hand: --
decorated with gold, and Grendel's hand: --

"For the sight I see to the Sovran Ruler
"For the sight I see I give the Sovereign Ruler [God]

be speedy thanks! A throng of sorrows
spedy thanks! A collection of sorrows

I have borne from Grendel; but God still works
I have suffered from Grendel; but God still works

wonder on wonder, the Warden-of-Glory.
wonders, the Guardian of Glory.

It was but now that I never more
It was only now that I never more

for woes that weighed on me waited help
needed help for woes that weighed on me

long as I lived, when, laved in blood,
long as I lived, when, washed in blood,

stood sword-gore-stained this stateliest house, --
stood red-stained this stateliest house, --

widespread woe for wise men all,
widespread woe for all men,

who had no hope to hinder ever
who had no hope to ever prevent

foes infernal and fiendish sprites

hellish foes and fiendish creatures

from havoc in hall. This hero now,

from causing chaos in the hall. This hero now,

by the Wielder's might, a work has done

by God's power, has done a deed

that not all of us erst could ever do

that none of us could ever do before

by wile and wisdom. Lo, well can she say

by cleverness and wisdom. Indeed, she can surely say

whoso of women this warrior bore

whatever woman birthed this warrior

among sons of men, if still she liveth,

among sons of men, if she is still alive,

that the God of the ages was good to her

that God was good to her

in the birth of her bairn. Now, Beowulf, thee,

in the birth of her son. Now, Beowulf, you,

of heroes best, I shall heartily love

best of heroes, I shall heartily love

as mine own, my son; preserve thou ever

as my own son; maintain forever

 this kinship new: thou shalt never lack

this new connection between us: you shall never be without

wealth of the world that I wield as mine!

wealth of the world that I use as mine!

Full oft for less have I largess showered,

Often for less I have showered riches,

my precious hoard, on a punier man,

my precious hoard, on a lesser man,

less stout in struggle. Thyself hast now

not as accomplished in action. You have now

fulfilled such deeds, that thy fame shall endure

fulfilled such deeds, that your fame shall endure

through all the ages. As ever he did,

for the rest of time. As he always has,

well may the Wielder reward thee still!"

may God reward you well still!"

Beowulf spake, bairn of Ecgtheow: --

Beowulf spoke, child of Ecgtheow: --

"This work of war most willingly

"This work of war fully willingly

we have fought, this fight, and fearlessly dared

we have fought this fight and fearlessly braved

force of the foe. Fain, too, were I

the danger of the demon. Definitely, too, was I

hadst thou but seen himself, what time

had you only seen him, what time

the fiend in his trappings tottered to fall!

it took for the fiend to totter and fall!

Swiftly, I thought, in strongest gripe

Swiftly, I though, in the strongest of grips

on his bed of death to bind him down,

to bring him down to death,

that he in the hent of this hand of mine

that he being crushed by this hand of mine

should breathe his last: but he broke away.

should breathe for the last time: but broke away.

Him I might not -- the Maker willed not --

Him I was not able -- God decided it would not be --

hinder from flight, and firm enough hold

to prevent from fleeing, and firm enough hold

the life-destroyer: too sturdy was he,

the killer: he was too sturdy,

the ruthless, in running! For rescue, however,

the ruthless one, in running! While escaping, however,

he left behind him his hand in pledge,

he left behind his hand as a price,

arm and shoulder; nor aught of help

arm and shoulder; no kind of help

could the cursed one thus procure at all.

could the cursed one find at all in this way.

None the longer liveth he, loathsome fiend,

He lives no longer, loathsome fiend,

sunk in his sins, but sorrow holds him

lost to his sins, but sorrow holds him

tightly grasped in gripe of anguish,

tightly grasped in the grip of anguish,

in baleful bonds, where bide he must,

in awful chains, where he must suffer,

evil outlaw, such awful doom

the evil outlaw, such an awful doom

as the Mighty Maker shall mete him out.

as God should give him.

More silent seemed the son of Ecglaf

The son of Ecglaf [Unferth] was silent then

in boastful speech of his battle-deeds,

no longer boasting about his own battle-deeds,

since athelings all, through the earl's great prowess,

since all the warriors, through the noble's [Beowulf's] great ability,

beheld that hand, on the high roof gazing,

saw that hand, gazing on the high roof,

foeman's fingers, -- the forepart of each

the enemy's fingers, -- the front part of each

of the sturdy nails to steel was likest, --

of the sturdy nails was like steel, --

heathen's "hand-spear," hostile warrior's

the monster's "hand-spear," the hostile warrior's

claw uncanny. 'Twas clear, they said,

supernatural claw. It was clear, they said,

that him no blade of the brave could touch,

that no [sword] blade of the brave could touch him,

how keen soever, or cut away

no matter how sharp, or cut away

that battle-hand bloody from baneful foe.
that bloody battle-hand from the evil foe.

~*~

Section XV

THERE was hurry and hest in Heorot now

THERE was hurry and bustle in Heorot now

for hands to bedeck it, and dense was the throng

for hands to beautify it, and the crowd was dense

of men and women the wine-hall to cleanse,

of men and women to clean the wine-hall,

the guest-room to garnish. Gold-gay shone the hangings

and to decorate the guest-room. The hangings were cheerful with gold

that were wove on the wall, and wonders many
that were woven on the wall, and many wonders

to delight each mortal that looks upon them.

to delight each person that looks upon them.

Though braced within by iron bands,

Though reinforced inside by iron bands,

that building bright was broken sorely;

the bright building was badly broken;

rent were its hinges; the roof alone

its hinges were ripped; only the roof

held safe and sound, when, seared with crime,

held safe and solid, when, burned by his crime,

the fiendish foe his flight essayed,
the fiendish foe had fled,

of life despairing. -- No light thing that,
giving up on life. -- It was no light thing,

the flight for safety, -- essay it who will!
that run for safety, -- ponder it who wishes!

Forced of fate, he shall find his way
Forced by fate, he shall find his way

to the refuge ready for race of man,
to the afterlife ready for humankind,

for soul-possessors, and sons of earth;
for those with souls, the children of earth;

and there his body on bed of death
and there his body, finally dead

shall rest after revel.
shall rest after life's enjoyment.

Arrived was the hour
The hour was here

when to hall proceeded Healfdene's son:

when Healfdene's son went to the hall:

the king himself would sit to banquet.

the king would sit to feast.

Ne'er heard I of host in haughtier throng

Never have I heard of a more high-born crowd,

more graciously gathered round giver-of-rings!

more graciously gathered around a royal!

Bowed then to bench those bearers-of-glory,

Sitting then those bearers-of-glory,

fain of the feasting. Featly received

joining in the feast. Fairly received

many a mead-cup the mighty-in-spirit,

many a drink of mead, those mighty in spirit,

kinsmen who sat in the sumptuous hall,

family members who sat in the fancy hall,

Hrothgar and Hrothulf. Heorot now

Hrothgar and Hrothulf. Heorot was now

was filled with friends; the folk of Scyldings

filled with friends; the people of Scyld

ne'er yet had tried the traitor's deed.

had never yet tried treachery.

To Beowulf gave the bairn of Healfdene

The son of Healfdene gave Beowulf

a gold-wove banner, guerdon of triumph,

a banner woven with gold, a token of triumph,

broidered battle-flag, breastplate and helmet;

embroidered battle-flag, a breastplate, a helmet,

and a splendid sword was seen of many

and a splendid sword, as many saw

borne to the brave one. Beowulf took

given to the brave one. Beowulf took

cup in hall: for such costly gifts

drink in the hall: for such expensive gifts

he suffered no shame in that soldier throng.
he was not ashamed to receive in that crowd of soldiers.

For I heard of few heroes, in heartier mood,

For I have heard of few happier heroes,

with four such gifts, so fashioned with gold,

with four such gifts, made with gold in that way,

on the ale-bench honoring others thus!

on the ale-bench honoring others in such a way!

O'er the roof of the helmet high, a ridge,

Over the top of the high helmet, a ridge,

wound with wires, kept ward o'er the head,

wound with wires, guarded the head,

lest the relict-of-files should fierce invade,

in case a monster should try to invade,

sharp in the strife, when that shielded hero

fierce in the fight, when that shielded hero

should go to grapple against his foes.

would go to wrestle against his foes.

Then the earls'-defence on the floor bade lead

Then the defender of the nobles led

coursers eight, with carven head-gear,

eight warhorses and riders, with carved head-gear,

adown the hall: one horse was decked

down the hall: one horse was dressed

with a saddle all shining and set in jewels;

with a shining, jeweled saddle;

'twas the battle-seat of the best of kings,

it was the battle-seat of the best of kings,

when to play of swords the son of Healfdene

when to fighting with swords the son of Healfdene

was fain to fare. Ne'er failed his valor

went to do. His valor never failed

in the crush of combat when corpses fell.

in the crush of combat when men became corpses.

To Beowulf over them both then gave

Both then gave to Beowulf

the refuge-of-Ingwines right and power,

the rights and powers of the royal family,

o'er war-steeds and weapons: wished him joy of them.

over the warhorses and weapons: wished him happiness with them.

Manfully thus the mighty prince,
Generously, in this way the mighty prince,

hoard-guard for heroes, that hard fight repaid

guardian of treasure for heroes, repaid that hard fight

with steeds and treasures contemned by none

with horses and treasures condemned by none

who is willing to say the sooth aright.
who is willing to tell the honest truth.

~*~

Section XVI

AND the lord of earls, to each that came

AND the king, to each man that came

with Beowulf over the briny ways,

with Beowulf over the salty seas,

an heirloom there at the ale-bench gave,

gave an heirloom at the ale-bench,

precious gift; and the price bade pay

a precious gift; and paid the price

in gold for him whom Grendel erst

in gold for each man whom Grendel previously

murdered, -- and fain of them more had killed,

murdered, -- had he would have killed more of them,

had not wisest God their Wyrd averted,

had wisest God not prevented their fate,

and the man's brave mood. The Maker then

and also Beowulf's bravery. God then

ruled human kind, as here and now.

ruled humanity, as he does here and now.

Therefore is insight always best,

Therefore wisdom is always best,

and forethought of mind. How much awaits him

along with planning. Much waits for him

of lief and of loath, who long time here,

both good and bad, who for a long time

through days of warfare this world endures!
endures this world and its days of war!

Then song and music mingled sounds

Then song and music mixed together

in the presence of Healfdene's head-of-armies

in the presence of Healfdene's leader

and harping was heard with the hero-lay

and harp music was heard with the heroic epic

as Hrothgar's singer the hall-joy woke

as Hrothgar's singer pleased the hall

along the mead-seats, making his song

all along the benches, making his song

of that sudden raid on the sons of Finn.

of that sudden attack on the sons of Finn.

Healfdene's hero, Hnaef the Scylding,

Healfdene's hero, Hnaef the Scyld,

was fated to fall in the Frisian slaughter.

was destined to die in the battle of Fris.

Hildeburh needed not hold in value

Hildeburh did not need to value

her enemies' honor! Innocent both

her enemies' honor! They were both innocent,

were the loved ones she lost at the linden-play,

the loved ones she lost at the fight,

bairn and brother, they bowed to fate,

son and brother, they accepted their fate,

stricken by spears; 'twas a sorrowful woman!

struck by spears; she was a sorrowful woman!

None doubted why the daughter of Hoc

No one wondered why the daughter of Hoc

bewailed her doom when dawning came,

cried over her doom when dawn came,

and under the sky she saw them lying,

and she saw them lying under the sky,

kinsmen murdered, where most she had kenned

murdered family, who she had considered best

of the sweets of the world! By war were swept, too,

of all the good things in the world! By war were affected, too,

Finn's own liegemen, and few were left;

Finn's own loyal men, and few were left;

in the parleying-place he could ply no longer

he could no longer make a diplomatic compromise,

weapon, nor war could he wage on Hengest,

or go against Hengest with any kind of weapon,

and rescue his remnant by right of arms

and rescue what was left by his fighting

from the prince's thane. A pact he offered:

from the prince's nobleman. He offered a truce agreement:

another dwelling the Danes should have,

the Danes could have another piece of land,

hall and high-seat, and half the power

a hall and throne, and half the power

should fall to them in Frisian land;

of the Frisian land would go to them;

and at the fee-gifts, Folcwald's son
and as for rewards, Foclwald's son

day by day the Danes should honor,
would honor the Danes every day,

the folk of Hengest favor with rings,
the people Hengest valued with rings,

even as truly, with treasure and jewels,
even as, indeed, with treasure and jewels,

with fretted gold, as his Frisian kin
with worked gold, as his Frisian kin

he meant to honor in ale-hall there.
he meant to give gifts in the ale-hall there.

Pact of peace they plighted further
They made more peace treaties

on both sides firmly. Finn to Hengest
firmly on both sides. Finn to Hengest

with oath, upon honor, openly promised
swore, upon honor, and openly promised

that woful remnant, with wise-men's aid,
that the sad survivors, with the aid of wise men,

nobly to govern, so none of the guests

he would govern nobly, so that none of the guests

by word or work should warp the treaty,

would violate the treaty by word or action,

or with malice of mind bemoan themselves

or with malicious thoughts complain that they

as forced to follow their fee-giver's slayer,

were forced to follow their ruler's killer,

lordless men, as their lot ordained.

considering themselves fated to be without a lord.

Should Frisian, moreover, with foeman's taunt,

Additionally, if a Frisian, with the insults of an enemy,

that murderous hatred to mind recall,

bring to mind that murderous hatred,

then edge of the sword must seal his doom.
then he must be executed by the sword.

Oaths were given, and ancient gold

Promises were made, and ancient gold

heaped from hoard. -- The hardy Scylding,

piled from the hoard. -- The hardy Scylding,

battle-thane best, on his balefire lay.

the best of noble warriors, was cremated.

All on the pyre were plain to see

All on the funeral bonfire were easily seen

the gory sark, the gilded swine-crest,

the bloodstained flag, the gold-decorated picture of a boar,

boar of hard iron, and athelings many

the boar of hard iron, and many warriors

slain by the sword: at the slaughter they fell.

killed by the sword: at the massacre they fell.

It was Hildeburh's hest, at Hnaef's own pyre

It was Hildeburh who insisted, at Hnaef's own funeral bonfire,

the bairn of her body on brands to lay,

to place the body of her own son,

his bones to burn, on the balefire placed,

his bones to burn, placed on the flames,

at his uncle's side. In sorrowful dirges

at his uncle's side. In sorrowful songs

bewept them the woman: great wailing ascended.

the women wept: loud crying rose up from them.

Then wound up to welkin the wildest of death-fires,

Then the wildest of the death-fires shot into the sky,

roared o'er the hillock: heads all were melted,

roared over the hill tops: their heads were all melted,

gashes burst, and blood gushed out

their wounds burst with gushing blood

from bites of the body. Balefire devoured,

from injuries of the body. The fire devoured,

greediest spirit, those spared not by war

that greedy spirit, those that were taken by war

out of either folk: their flower was gone.
out of both sides: their life was gone.

~*~

Section XVII

THEN hastened those heroes their home to see,

THEN the heroes hurried home to see,

friendless, to find the Frisian land,

all alone, to find the Frisian land,

houses and high burg. Hengest still

houses and tall city. Hengest still

through the death-dyed winter dwelt with Finn,

lived with Finn through the death-filled winter,

holding pact, yet of home he minded,

honoring the treaty, yet he missed home,

though powerless his ring-decked prow to drive

though his ring-decorated ship was powerless to sail

over the waters, now waves rolled fierce

over the sea, now that waves rolled fierce

lashed by the winds, or winter locked them

whipped up by the winds, or winter locked them

in icy fetters. Then fared another

in icy chains. Then cam another

year to men's dwellings, as yet they do,

year to men's homes, as they still do,

the sunbright skies, that their season ever

in the skies bright with sun, that their season forever

duly await. Far off winter was driven;

they naturally wait for. Winter was driven far off;

fair lay earth's breast; and fain was the rover,

the earth was beautiful; and the traveler wished,

the guest, to depart, though more gladly he pondered

the guest wished, to depart, though he pondered more gladly

on wreaking his vengeance than roaming the deep,

on having his revenge than on roaming the seas,

and how to hasten the hot encounter

and how to hurry the angry encounter

where sons of the Frisians were sure to be.

where Frisian warriors were sure to be.

So he escaped not the common doom,

So he did not escape the doom others had,

when Hun with "Lafing," the light-of-battle,

when Hun with his sword, named "Lafing," the light-of battle, best of blades, his bosom pierced:

best of blades, stabbed his heart:

its edge was famed with the Frisian earls.

its edge was famous among the Frisian earls.

On fierce-heart Finn there fell likewise,

The fierce-heart Finn killed himself then,

on himself at home, the horrid sword-death;

at home, with a horrible sword-death'

for Guthlaf and Oslaf of grim attack

because Guthlaf and Oslaf had sorrowfully told him

had sorrowing told, from sea-ways landed,

of grim attack, when they arrived from their sea voyage,

mourning their woes. Finn's wavering spirit

mourning their losses. Finn's unsure spirit

bode not in breast. The burg was reddened

had left his body. The city was reddened

with blood of foemen, and Finn was slain,

with the blood of enemies, and Finn was killed,

king amid clansmen; the queen was taken.

the king among his clan; the queen was taken.

To their ship the Scylding warriors bore

The Scylding warriors took to the ship

all the chattels the chieftain owned,

all the valuables the chieftain owned,

whatever they found in Finn's domain

anything found in Finn's domain

of gems and jewels. The gentle wife

that was gems and jewels. The gentle wife

o'er paths of the deep to the Danes they bore,

they took over the sea to the Danes,

led to her land.

leading her to her land.

The lay was finished,

The epic was finished,

the gleeman's song. Then glad rose the revel;

the minstrel's song. The celebration continued gladly,

bench-joy brightened. Bearers draw

the guests joyful. The servers fetched

from their "wonder-vats" wine. Comes Wealhtheow forth,

wine from their vats. Wealhtheow came forth,

under gold-crown goes where the good pair sit,

under her golden crown she went where the good pair sat,

uncle and nephew, true each to the other one,

uncle and nephew, loyal to one another,

kindred in amity. Unferth the spokesman

loving family. Unferth the spokesman

at the Scylding lord's feet sat: men had faith in his spirit,

sat at the Scylding lord's feet: men had faith in his spirit,

his keenness of courage, though kinsmen had found him

the strength of his courage, though kinsmen had found him

unsure at the sword-play. The Scylding queen spoke:

not the best with a sword. The Scylding queen spoke:

"Quaff of this cup, my king and lord,

"Drink of this cup, my king and lord,

breaker of rings, and blithe be thou,

breaker of rings, and be carefree,

gold-friend of men; to the Geats here speak

great friend of men; speak to the Geats here

such words of mildness as man should use.

such pleasant words as a man should use.

Be glad with thy Geats; of those gifts be mindful,

Be glad with your Geatish men; treasure your gifts,

or near or far, which now thou hast.

near or far, which you have now.

Men say to me, as son thou wishest

Men say to me, as a son you wish

yon hero to hold. Thy Heorot purged,

to hold that hero there. Your Heorot is rid of Grendel,

jewel-hall brightest, enjoy while thou canst,

your brightest jeweled hall, enjoy it while you can;

with many a largess; and leave to thy kin

with great generosity; and leave to your kin

folk and realm when forth thou goest

your people and kingdom when you go forth

to greet thy doom. For gracious I deem

into death. For I consider gracious

my Hrothulf, willing to hold and rule

my Hrothulf, who is willing to hold and rule

nobly our youths, if thou yield up first,

our youths nobly, if you willingly give up first,

prince of Scyldings, thy part in the world.

prince of Scyldings, your part in the world [when you die].

I ween with good he will well requite

I believe he will repay with good

offspring of ours, when all he minds

our children, when he remembers

that for him we did in his helpless days

what we did for him in his helpless days

of gift and grace to gain him honor!"

the gifts and the grace to gain him honor!"

Then she turned to the seat where her sons were placed,

Then she turned to the seat where her sons sat,

Hrethric and Hrothmund, with heroes' bairns,

Hrethric and Hrothmund, with heroes' children,

young men together: the Geat, too, sat there,

young men together: they sat with the Geat too,

Beowulf brave, the brothers between.

brave Beowulf, between the brothers.

~*~

Section XVIII

A CUP she gave him, with kindly greeting
SHE GAVE him a cup, with a kind greeting

and winsome words. Of wounden gold,
and sweet words. Of wound gold,

she offered, to honor him, arm-jewels twain,
she offered him two arm bands, to honor him,

corselet and rings, and of collars the noblest
bracelet and rings, and the noblest of necklaces

that ever I knew the earth around.
that I ever knew in all the earth.

Ne'er heard I so mighty, 'neath heaven's dome,
Never have I heard so large, beneath heaven,

a hoard-gem of heroes, since Hama bore
a hero's heap of gems, since Hama took

to his bright-built burg the Brisings' necklace,
to his bright city the Brisings' necklace,

jewel and gem casket. -- Jealousy fled he,
jewel and gem casket. -- He was escaping jealously,

Eormenric's hate: chose help eternal.
Eormenric's hate: he put himself in God's hands.

Hygelac Geat, grandson of Swerting,

Hygelac the Geat, Swerting's grandson,

on the last of his raids this ring bore with him,

carried this ring with him on the last of his raids,

under his banner the booty defending,

under his flag defending the treasure,

the war-spoil warding; but Wyrd o'erwhelmed him

guarding the war prize; but Fate overwhelmed him

what time, in his daring, dangers he sought,

what time, in his recklesness, he looked for danger,

feud with Frisians. Fairest of gems

fighting with Frisian. The most beautiful of gems,

he bore with him over the beaker-of-waves,

he carried with him over the ocean,

sovran strong: under shield he died.

a strong sovereing: he died in battle.

Fell the corpse of the king into keeping of Franks,

The corpse of the king fell into the hands of Franks,

gear of the breast, and that gorgeous ring;

his armor, and that gorgeous ring;

weaker warriors won the spoil,

weaker warriors won the prize,

after gripe of battle, from Geatland's lord,

after the grip of battle, from Geatland's lord,

and held the death-field.

and won the skirmish.

Din rose in hall.

The hall became even louder.

Wealhtheow spake amid warriors, and said: --

Wealhtheow spoke among warriors, and said: --

"This jewel enjoy in thy jocund youth,

"Enjoy this jewel in your jolly youth,

Beowulf lov'd, these battle-weeds wear,

beloved Beowulf, these battle clothes wear,

a royal treasure, and richly thrive!

a royal treasure, and thrive richly!

Preserve thy strength, and these striplings here

Preserve your strength, and these young men here

counsel in kindness: requital be mine.

rule in kindness: I will reward you.

Hast done such deeds, that for days to come

You have done such deeds, that for years to come

thou art famed among folk both far and near,

you will be famous among people both far and near,

so wide as washeth the wave of Ocean

so wide as the ocean's waves wash

his windy walls. Through the ways of life

their windy walls. Through the ways of life

prosper, O prince! I pray for thee

prosper, Oh prince! I wish for you

rich possessions. To son of mine

rich possessions. To my son

be helpful in deed and uphold his joys!

be helpful in deed and work for his happiness!

Here every earl to the other is true,

Here every nobleman is faithful to the others,

mild of mood, to the master loyal!

kind and generous, loyal to the master!

Thanes are friendly, the throng obedient,

High-born men are friendly, the people obedient,

liegemen are revelling: list and obey!"

servants are celebrating: listen and obey!"

Went then to her place. -- That was proudest of feasts;

She went back to her rooms. -- That was the greatest of feass;

flowed wine for the warriors. Wyrd they knew not,

wine flowed for the warriors. They did not know Fate,

destiny dire, and the doom to be seen

the dark destiny, and the doom to be seen

by many an earl when eve should come,

by many a man when evening should come,

and Hrothgar homeward hasten away,

and Hrothgar hurried away to home,

royal, to rest. The room was guarded

the royal to rest. The room was guarded

by an army of earls, as erst was done.

by an army of nobles, as had been done before.

They bared the bench-boards; abroad they spread

They cleared the benches and tables; on top they spread

beds and bolsters. -- One beer-carouser

beds and blankets. -- One drunk celebrator

in danger of doom lay down in the hall. --

in danger of doom lay down. --

At their heads they set their shields of war,

Next to their heads they placed their war shields,

bucklers bright; on the bench were there

bright battle gear; on the bench were there

over each atheling, easy to see,

over each warrior, easily seen,

the high battle-helmet, the haughty spear,

their tall battle-helmets, their proud spears,

the corselet of rings. 'Twas their custom so

the bracelets of arm-rings. It was their custom

ever to be for battle prepared,

to always be prepared for battle,

at home, or harrying, which it were,

at home, or traveling, whichever it was,

even as oft as evil threatened

whenever evil would happen to threaten

their sovran king. -- They were clansmen good.

their sovereign king. -- They were good clansmen.

Section XIX

THEN sank they to sleep. With sorrow one bought

THEY then fell asleep. One paid for

his rest of the evening, -- as ofttime had happened

his rest that night with sorrow, -- as often happened

when Grendel guarded that golden hall,

when Grendel attacked that golded hall,

evil wrought, till his end drew nigh,

and did evil, until his death came near,

slaughter for sins. 'Twas seen and told

slaughter for sins. It was seen and told

how an avenger survived the fiend,

how one survived the fiend, to avenge him,

as was learned afar. The livelong time

as was learned far away. The entire time

after that grim fight, Grendel's mother,

after that unpleasant fight, Grendel's mother,

monster of women, mourned her woe.

monster of women, mourned her grief.

She was doomed to dwell in the dreary waters,

She was doomed to live in the stagnant waters,

cold sea-courses, since Cain cut down
cold currents, since Cain killed

with edge of the sword his only brother,
with a sword his only brother,

his father's offspring: outlawed he fled,
his father's offspring: he ran, exiled,

marked with murder, from men's delights
marked with murder, from the joys of life,

warded the wilds. -- There woke from him
wandered the wilderness. -- Descended from him

such fate-sent ghosts as Grendel, who,
were such ghosts sent by fate as Grendel, who,

war-wolf horrid, at Heorot found
a horrible monster, found at Heorot

a warrior watching and waiting the fray,
a warrior watching and waiting to fight,

with whom the grisly one grappled amain.
with whom the violent villain wrestled.

But the man remembered his mighty power,

But the man remembered his great strength,

the glorious gift that God had sent him,

the glorious gift sent by God,

in his Maker's mercy put his trust

put his trust in God's mercy

for comfort and help: so he conquered the foe,

for comfort and help: so he overcame Grendel,

felled the fiend, who fled abject,

killed the monster, who fled pathetically,

reft of joy, to the realms of death,

having lost all joy, to the places of death,

mankind's foe. And his mother now,

humanity's enemy. And his mother now,

gloomy and grim, would go that quest

gloomy and grim, would go on a quest

of sorrow, the death of her son to avenge.

of sorrow, to avenge her son's death.

To Heorot came she, where helmeted Danes

She came to Heorot, where helmeted Danes

slept in the hall. Too soon came back

slept in the hall. She came back too soon

old ills of the earls, when in she burst,

old trouble of the nobles, when she burst in,

the mother of Grendel. Less grim, though, that terror,

Grendel's mother. Her terror was less grim,

e'en as terror of woman in war is less,

even as the terror of a woman warrior is less,

might of maid, than of men in arms

the strength of a female, than of men with weapons

when, hammer-forged, the falchion hard,

when, forged with hammers, the hard hilt,

sword gore-stained, through swine of the helm,

bloody sword, through the symbol of the wild boar,

crested, with keen blade carves amain.

decorated, with sharp blade stabs wildly.

Then was in hall the hard-edge drawn,
There were many sharp edges in the hall,

the swords on the settles, and shields a-many

many swords and shields rested there,

firm held in hand: nor helmet minded

firmly held in hands: but did not mind helmets

nor harness of mail, whom that horror seized.

or chain-mail, whom that horror [Grendel's mother] grabbed.

Haste was hers; she would hie afar

She hurried; she would run far away

and save her life when the liegemen saw her.

and save her life when the men saw her.

Yet a single atheling up she seized

Yet she picked up a single warrior

fast and firm, as she fled to the moor.

tightly and firmly, as she fled to the moor.

He was for Hrothgar of heroes the dearest,

He was the dearest of heroes to Hrothgar,

of trusty vassals betwixt the seas,

best of the trusty vassals between the seas,

whom she killed on his couch, a clansman famous,

whom she killed on his bed, a famous clansman,

in battle brave. -- Nor was Beowulf there;

brave in battle. -- Beowulf was not there;

another house had been held apart,

for another house had been reserved,

after giving of gold, for the Geat renowned. --

after giving him the gold, for the renowned Geat. --

Uproar filled Heorot; the hand all had viewed,

All Heorot was in uproar; that hand everyone had seen,

blood-flecked, she bore with her; bale was returned,

blood-flecked, she carried off with her; trouble had returned,

dole in the dwellings: 'twas dire exchange

a price to be paid at home: it was an awful exchange

where Dane and Geat were doomed to give

where both tribes were doomed to give up

the lives of loved ones. Long-tried king,

the lives of loved ones. Longsuffering king,

the hoary hero, at heart was sad

the great hero, was sad at heart

when he knew his noble no more lived,

when he knew his noble lived no more,

and dead indeed was his dearest thane.

and his dearest thane was dead indeed.

To his bower was Beowulf brought in haste,

Beowulf was brought to his bedroom in a great hurry,

dauntless victor. As daylight broke,

that dauntless winner. As daylight broke,

along with his earls the atheling lord,

along with his noblement the warrior lord,

with his clansmen, came where the king abode

with his clansmen, came where the king lived

waiting to see if the Wielder-of-All

waiting to see if Almighty God

would turn this tale of trouble and woe.

would stop all this trouble and woe.

Strode o'er floor the famed-in-strife,

Striding over the floor the famouse-in-fighting,

with his hand-companions, -- the hall resounded, --

with his right-hand-men, -- the hall filled with sound, --

wishing to greet the wise old king,

everyone wanting to greet the wise old king,

Ingwines' lord; he asked if the night

lord of Ingwines; he asked if the night

had passed in peace to the prince's mind.
had been peaceful for the prince.

~*~

Section XX

HROTHGAR spake, helmet-of-Scyldings: --

HROTHGAR spoke, he who led the Scyldings: --

"Ask not of pleasure! Pain is renewed

"Do not ask about pleasure! Pain has returned

to Danish folk. Dead is Aeschere,

to the Danish people. Aeshere is dead,

of Yrmenlaf the elder brother,

the elder brother of Yrmenlaf,

my sage adviser and stay in council,

my wise adviser and representative in council,

shoulder-comrade in stress of fight

a right-hand man in the stress of fight

when warriors clashed and we warded our heads,

when warriors clashed their swords and we guarded our heads,

hewed the helm-boars; hero famed

carved the boars on our armor; a famous hero

should be every earl as Aeschere was!

every noble should be as Aeschere was!

But here in Heorot a hand hath slain him

But here in Heorot a hand has killed him

of wandering death-sprite. I wot not whither,

a wandering death-spirit. I do not know where,

proud of the prey, her path she took,

proud of her prey, what path she took,

fain of her fill. The feud she avenged

after taking her fill. The feud she avenged,

that yesternight, unyieldingly,

that the night before last, without mercy,

Grendel in grimmest grasp thou killedst, --

you killed Grendel in grimmest grasp, --

seeing how long these liegemen mine

seeing how long these loyal men of mine

he ruined and ravaged. Reft of life,

he killed and ate. Losing his life,

in arms he fell. Now another comes,

he died. Now another one comes,

keen and cruel, her kin to avenge,

eager and cruel, to avenge her son,

faring far in feud of blood:

coming far in feud of blood:

so that many a thane shall think, who e'er

so that many a thane shall think, who ever

sorrows in soul for that sharer of rings,

is sad in their soul for that nobleman,

this is hardest of heart-bales. The hand lies low

this is the hardest of heart burdens. The hand lies low

that once was willing each wish to please.

that was once so willing to please.

Land-dwellers here and liegemen mine,

People of this land and loyal men of mine,

who house by those parts, I have heard relate

who live near here, I have heard tell

that such a pair they have sometimes seen,

that they have sometimes seen a pair like this:

march-stalkers mighty the moorland haunting,

large stalkers haunting the moorland,

wandering spirits: one of them seemed,

wandering creatures: one of them seemed,

so far as my folk could fairly judge,

so far as my people could fairly judge,

of womankind; and one, accursed,

to be female; and one, the cursed,

in man's guise trod the misery-track

walked the misery-track in the form of a man,

of exile, though huger than human bulk.

in exile, though he was huger than a normal human.

Grendel in days long gone they named him,

They named him Grendel long ago,

folk of the land; his father they knew not,

the people of the land; they did not know his father,

nor any brood that was born to him

nor any children that he had

of treacherous spirits. Untrod is their home;

of treacherous spirits. No one goes to their home;

by wolf-cliffs haunt they and windy headlands,

they live by wild cliffs and windy headlands,

fenways fearful, where flows the stream

fearful woods, where the stream flows

from mountains gliding to gloom of the rocks,

from mountains, gliding to the gloomy rocks,

underground flood. Not far is it hence

underground flood. Not far from there

in measure of miles that the mere expands,

in miles, the swamp expands,

and o'er it the frost-bound forest hanging,

and over it the frost-covered forest hanging,

sturdily rooted, shadows the wave.

rooted firmly, casts shadows over the water.

By night is a wonder weird to see,

By night there is a strange sight,

fire on the waters. So wise lived none

fire on the waters [marsh gas flames]. No one has lived

of the sons of men, to search those depths!

no one human, to explore those depths!

Nay, though the heath-rover, harried by dogs,

No, even if a beast being hunted by dogs,

the horn-proud hart, this holt should seek,

the proud deer stag, should come to this place,

long distance driven, his dear life first

being driven by dogs, his dear life first

on the brink he yields ere he brave the plunge

he is willing to give up rather than brave the plunge

to hide his head: 'tis no happy place!

to hide his head: it is no happy place!

Thence the welter of waters washes up

From there the water washes up

wan to welkin when winds bestir

dark into the sky when the winds stir up

evil storms, and air grows dusk,

evil storms, and the air goes dusky,

and the heavens weep. Now is help once more

and the heavens pour rain. Now, again, we can look for help

with thee alone! The land thou knowst not,

from you alone! You do not know the land,

place of fear, where thou findest out

that place of fear, where you find

that sin-flecked being. Seek if thou dare!

that sin-stained being. Go if you dare!

I will reward thee, for waging this fight,

I will reward you, for fighting this fight,

with ancient treasure, as erst I did,

with ancient treasure, as previously I did,

with winding gold, if thou winnest back."

with gold, if you win and return."

~*~

Section XXI

BEOWULF spake, bairn of Ecgtheow:

BEOWULF spoke, the son of Ecgtheow:

"Sorrow not, sage! It beseems us better

"Do not be sad, wise one! It is better for us

friends to avenge than fruitlessly mourn them.

to avenge friends than to mourn them pointlessly.

Each of us all must his end abide
Each of us must all die one day

in the ways of the world; so win who may

by the ways of the world; so achieve who may

glory ere death! When his days are told,

glory before death! When his life is said and done,

that is the warrior's worthiest doom.

that is the warrior's best goal.

Rise, O realm-warder! Ride we anon,

Rise, Oh king! We will ride now

and mark the trail of the mother of Grendel.

and follow the trail of Grendel's mother.

No harbor shall hide her -- heed my promise! --

No harbor shall hide her -- listen to my promise! --

enfolding of field or forested mountain

the shelter of a field or a forested mountain

or floor of the flood, let her flee where she will!

or even the bottom of the lake, let her flee where she wants!

But thou this day endure in patience,

If you only endure today in patience,

as I ween thou wilt, thy woes each one."

as I believe you will, each one of your woes."

Leaped up the graybeard: God he thanked,

The old man leaped up: he thanked God,

mighty Lord, for the man's brave words.

the Almighty, for Beowulf's brave words.

For Hrothgar soon a horse was saddled

A horse was soon saddled for Hrothgar

wave-maned steed. The sovran wise

a steed with a rippled mane. The wise sovereign

stately rode on; his shield-armed men

rode on in state; his shield-armed men

followed in force. The footprints led

followed him forcefully. The footprints led

along the woodland, widely seen,

along the woodland, easily seen,

a path o'er the plain, where she passed, and trod

a path over the plain, where she passed, and walked

the murky moor; of men-at-arms

the murky moor; of soldiers

she bore the bravest and best one, dead,

she carried off the bravest and best one, dead,

him who with Hrothgar the homestead ruled.

he who ruled the homestead with Hrothgar.

On then went the atheling-born

Onward went the warrior-born

o'er stone-cliffs steep and strait defiles,

over steep stone cliffs and steeper slopes,

narrow passes and unknown ways,

narrow passes and mysterious ways,

headlands sheer, and the haunts of the Nicors.

sheer headlands, and the habitat of the water demons.

Foremost he fared, a few at his side

He went first, a few at his side

of the wiser men, the ways to scan,

of the wiser men, to keep a lookout,

till he found in a flash the forested hill

until he found, suddenly, the forested hill

hanging over the hoary rock,

hanging over the sturdy rock,

a woful wood: the waves below

a melancholy wood: the waves below

were dyed in blood. The Danish men

were colored with blood. The Danish men

had sorrow of soul, and for Scyldings all,

were sorrowful, and for all Scyldings,

for many a hero, 'twas hard to bear,

for many heroes, it was hard to bear,

ill for earls, when Aeschere's head

terrible for the nobles, when Aeschere's head

they found by the flood on the foreland there.

they found by the water there.

Waves were welling, the warriors saw,
Waves were rising, the warriors saw,

hot with blood; but the horn sang oft
hot with blood; but the horn called out often

battle-song bold. The band sat down,
a bold battle-song. The band sat down,

and watched on the water worm-like things,
and watched worm-like things on the water,

sea-dragons strange that sounded the deep,
strange sea-dragons diving deep,

and nicors that lay on the ledge of the ness --
and water demons that lay on the edge of the lake --

such as oft essay at hour of morn
such as often emerge in the morning

on the road-of-sails their ruthless quest, --
to embark on their ruthless quests upon the water, --

and sea-snakes and monsters. These started away,
and sea-snakes and monsters. These darted away,

swollen and savage that song to hear,

savage and skittish to hear that song,

that war-horn's blast. The warden of Geats,

that war-horn's blast. The guardian of Geats,

with bolt from bow, then balked of life,

with arrow from his bow, then hit,

of wave-work, one monster, amid its heart

in the waves, one monster, in its heart

went the keen war-shaft; in water it seemed

went the sharp war-shaft; in water it seemed

less doughty in swimming whom death had seized.

feebler in swimming as it died.

Swift on the billows, with boar-spears well

Fast on the waves, with boar-spears well

hooked and barbed, it was hard beset,

hooked and barbed, it was heavily challenged,

done to death and dragged on the headland,

driven to death and dragged on the headland,

wave-roamer wondrous. Warriors viewed

the strange swimmer. Warriors viewed

the grisly guest. Then girt him Beowulf

the grisly creature. Then Beowulf put on

in martial mail, nor mourned for his life.

his chain mail, not fearing death.

His breastplate broad and bright of hues,

His broad and bright-colored breastplate,

woven by hand, should the waters try;

handwoven, if the waters tested it;

well could it ward the warrior's body

would do well protecting the warrior's body

that battle should break on his breast in vain

that an attack would attempt to hurt his chest in vain

nor harm his heart by the hand of a foe.

and the hand of foes could not harm his heart.

And the helmet white that his head protected

And the white helmet that protected his head

was destined to dare the deeps of the flood,

was destined to dive deep,

through wave-whirl win: 'twas wound with chains,

win throught the waves: it was wound with chains,

decked with gold, as in days of yore
decorated with gold, as in the olden days

the weapon-smith worked it wondrously,
the smith had worked it wonderfully,

with swine-forms set it, that swords nowise,
set with with boar symbols, so that no swords,

brandished in battle, could bite that helm.
brandished in battle, could harm that helmet.

Nor was that the meanest of mighty helps
That was not the least of the great assistance

which Hrothgar's orator offered at need:
which Hrothgar's spokesman offered at need:

"Hrunting" they named the hilted sword,
the named the hilted sword "Hrunting",

of old-time heirlooms easily first;
easily the best of old-time heirlooms;

iron was its edge, all etched with poison,
its edge was iron, its blade was poisoned,

with battle-blood hardened, nor blenched it at fight

hardened with battle-blood, and it did not fear to fight

in hero's hand who held it ever,

in any hero's hand that ever held it,

on paths of peril prepared to go

prepared to go on dangerous paths

to folkstead of foes. Not first time this

to the homeland of foes. This was not the first time

it was destined to do a daring task.

it was destined to do a brave thing.

For he bore not in mind, the bairn of Ecglaf

For the son of Ecglaf [Unferth] did not think

sturdy and strong, that speech he had made,

about that speech he had made,

drunk with wine, now this weapon he lent

when drunk with wine, now he lent this weapon

to a stouter swordsman. Himself, though, durst not

to a sturdier swordsman. He himself, though, did not dar

under welter of waters wager his life

to gamble his life under the waves

as loyal liegeman. So lost he his glory,

as a loyal man of the court. So he lost out on glory

honor of earls. With the other not so,

and the honor of the nobles. With the other [Beowulf] it was different,

who girded him now for the grim encounter.
who prepared himself now for the grim encounter.

~*~

Section XXII

BEOWULF spake, bairn of Ecgtheow: --

BEOWULF spoke, the child of Ecgtheow: --

"Have mind, thou honored offspring of Healfdene

"Keep in mind, you honored offspring of Healfdene

gold-friend of men, now I go on this quest,

great friend of men, now that I go on this quest,

sovran wise, what once was said:

sovereign wise, what was once said:

if in thy cause it came that I

if in your cause it happened that I

should lose my life, thou wouldst loyal bide

should lose my life, you would loyally honor

to me, though fallen, in father's place!

me, though fallen, in the place of a father!

Be guardian, thou, to this group of my thanes,

Be guardian, you, to this group of my noblemen,

my warrior-friends, if War should seize me;

my warrior-friends, if the fight should defeat me;

and the goodly gifts thou gavest me,

and the good gifts you gave me,

Hrothgar beloved, to Hygelac send!

beloved Hrothgar, send to Hygelac!

Geatland's king may ken by the gold,

Geatland's king may know by the gold,

Hrethel's son see, when he stares at the treasure,

Hrethel's son see, when he gazes upon the treasure,

that I got me a friend for goodness famed,
that I found myself a friend famous for goodness,

and joyed while I could in my jewel-bestower.

and found joy while I could in my jewel-giver.

And let Unferth wield this wondrous sword,

And let Unferth use this wonderful sword,

earl far-honored, this heirloom precious,

honored by so many nobles, this precious heirloom,

hard of edge: with Hrunting I

hard-edged: with Hrunting I

seek doom of glory, or Death shall take me."

will go gain glory, or Death shall take me."

After these words the Weder-Geat lord

After these words the lord of Weders and Geats

boldly hastened, biding never

boldly hurried, leaving no time

answer at all: the ocean floods

for any answer at all: the ocean floods

closed o'er the hero. Long while of the day

closed over the hero. A very long time

fled ere he felt the floor of the sea.

passed before he reached the sea floor.

Soon found the fiend who the flood-domain

She soon realized, that fiend who

sword-hungry held these hundred winters,

had heald this domain for a hundred years,

greedy and grim, that some guest from above,

greedy and grim, that some intruder from above,

some man, was raiding her monster-realm.

some man, was attacking her monster-realm.

She grasped out for him with grisly claws,

She reached out for him with grisly claws,

and the warrior seized; yet scathed she not

and grabbed the warrior; yet she did not wound

his body hale; the breastplate hindered,

his healthy body; the breastplate prevented

as she strove to shatter the sark of war,

as she tried to break the armor of war,

the linked harness, with loathsome hand.

the linked chain mail, with loathsome hand.

Then bore this brine-wolf, when bottom she touched,

Then she took, this monster, when she touched the bottom,

the lord of rings to the lair she haunted

she carried off the hero to the lair she haunted

whiles vainly he strove, though his valor held,

while he tried in vain, though bravely,

weapon to wield against wondrous monsters

to fight against amazing monsters

that sore beset him; sea-beasts many

that hunted him; many sea-beasts

tried with fierce tusks to tear his mail,

tried to tear his armor with fierce tusks,

and swarmed on the stranger. But soon he marked

and swarmed on the stranger. But soon he realized

he was now in some hall, he knew not which,

he was now in some hall, though he did not know which,

where water never could work him harm,

where there was no water to drown him,

nor through the roof could reach him ever

and wather could never reach him through the roof.

fangs of the flood. Firelight he saw,

He saw firelight,

beams of a blaze that brightly shone.

a bright blaze shining,

Then the warrior was ware of that wolf-of-the-deep,

And then the warrior was aware of that wolf-of-the-deep,

mere-wife monstrous. For mighty stroke

the monstrous wife of the lake. For with a mighty stroke

he swung his blade, and the blow withheld not.

he swung his blade, and did not hold back the blow.

Then sang on her head that seemly blade

The beautiful blade clanged on her head

its war-song wild. But the warrior found

its wild war-cry. But the warrior found

the light-of-battle was loath to bite,

this sword was being ineffective,

to harm the heart: its hard edge failed

refusing to harm the heart: its hard edge failed

the noble at need, yet had known of old

the noble who needed it, yet it had known before

strife hand to hand, and had helmets cloven,

hand-to-hand combat, and had sliced helmets in half,

doomed men's fighting-gear. First time, this,

destroyed men's armor. This was the first time

for the gleaming blade that its glory fell.

that the glory of this gleaming blade fell.

Firm still stood, nor failed in valor,

He still stood firmly, not failed in courage,

heedful of high deeds, Hygelac's kinsman;

heroic in deed, Hygelac's kindsman;

flung away fretted sword, featly jewelled,

he flung away the finely made sword, skillfully jeweled,

the angry earl; on earth it lay

the angry earl; it lay on the ground

steel-edged and stiff. His strength he trusted,

steel-edged and stiff. He trusted his strength,

hand-gripe of might. So man shall do

his hand-grip of power. So a man should do

whenever in war he weens to earn him

whenever in war he plans to earn himself

lasting fame, nor fears for his life!

lasting fame, and does not fear for his life!

Seized then by shoulder, shrank not from combat,

He seized then the shoulder, not shirking combat,

the Geatish war-prince Grendel's mother.

the Geatish war-prince grabbed Grendel's mother.

Flung then the fierce one, filled with wrath,

He flung then the fierce one, filled with rage,

his deadly foe, that she fell to ground.

his deadly foe, that she fell to the ground.

Swift on her part she paid him back

Quick on her part she paid him back

with grisly grasp, and grappled with him.

with a grisly grasp, and wrestled with him.

Spent with struggle, stumbled the warrior,

Exhausted with the struggle, the warrior stumbled,

fiercest of fighting-men, fell adown.

the fiercest of fighting-men fell down.

On the hall-guest she hurled herself,

She hurled herself on her guest,

hent her short sword, broad and brown-edged,

took her short sword, broad and brown-edged,

the bairn to avenge,

to avenge the child,

the sole-born son. -- On his shoulder lay

her only son. -- On his shoulder lay

braided breast-mail, barring death,

braided chain mail, saving him from death,

withstanding entrance of edge or blade.

withstanding the force of both edge and blade.

Life would have ended for Ecgtheow's son,

Life would have ended for Beowulf, son of Ecgtheow,

under wide earth for that earl of Geats,

under the earth for that noble of Geats,

had his armor of war not aided him,

had his war armor not helped him,

battle-net hard, and holy God

the hard battle-net, and holy God

wielded the victory, wisest Maker.

allowed the victory, wisest Maker.

The Lord of Heaven allowed his cause;

The Lord of Heaven took his side;

and easily rose the earl erect.
and the earl easily rose to his feet.

~*~

Section XXIII

'MID the battle-gear saw he a blade triumphant,

AMONG the battle-gear he saw a triumphant blade,

old-sword of Eotens, with edge of proof,

an old sword of Eotens, with a proven edge,

warriors' heirloom, weapon unmatched,

a warriors' heirloom, a weapon unmanted,

-- save only 'twas more than other men

-- it was more than other men

to bandy-of-battle could bear at all --

who could carry it into battle at all --

as the giants had wrought it, ready and keen.

as giants had crafted it, ready and sharp.

Seized then its chain-hilt the Scyldings' chieftain,

The Scyldings' chieftain seized it then,

bold and battle-grim, brandished the sword,

bold and grim, he brandished the sword,

reckless of life, and so wrathfully smote

reckless with his life, and so fiercely struck

that it gripped her neck and grasped her hard,

that it gripped her neck and hit her hard,

her bone-rings breaking: the blade pierced through

her spine breaking: the blade pierced through

that fated-one's flesh: to floor she sank.

that fiend's flesh, as fated: she sank to the floor.

Bloody the blade: he was blithe of his deed.

The blade was bloody: he was pleased with his success.

Then blazed forth light. 'Twas bright within

Then light blazed all around. It was as bright within

as when from the sky there shines unclouded

as when the sun shines unclouded from the sky.

heaven's candle. The hall he scanned.

He scanned the hall.

By the wall then went he; his weapon raised

He went by the wall; he raised his weapon

high by its hilts the Hygelac-thane,

high by its hilts, the noble of Hygelac,

angry and eager. That edge was not useless

angry and eager. That edge was still useful

to the warrior now. He wished with speed

to the warrior now. He wished that with speed

Grendel to guerdon for grim raids many,

Grendel would go to Hell for his many grim raids,

for the war he waged on Western-Danes

for the war he brought to Western-Danes

oftener far than an only time,

far more often than one time,

when of Hrothgar's hearth-companions

when of Hrothgar's friends and warriors

he slew in slumber, in sleep devoured,

he killed and devoured in their sleep,

fifteen men of the folk of Danes,

fifteen men of the Danish people,

and as many others outward bore,

and as many others he took way,

his horrible prey. Well paid for that

his horrible prey. He had paid for that, through

the wrathful prince! For now prone he saw

the righteously angry prince! For now he saw, lying

Grendel stretched there, spent with war,

Grendel stretched there, exhaused with war,

spoiled of life, so scathed had left him

now dead, so injured he had been

Heorot's battle. The body sprang far

in the battle at Heorot. The body [of Grendel's mother] went far

when after death it endured the blow,

when after death it took the blow,

sword-stroke savage, that severed its head.

the savage sword-stroke that severed its head.

Soon, then, saw the sage companions

Soon, then, the wise companions saw,

who waited with Hrothgar, watching the flood,

the ones who waited with Hrothgar, watching the waves,

that the tossing waters turbid grew,

that the tossing waters grew tempestuous,

blood-stained the mere. Old men together,

the lake blood-stained. Old men together,

hoary-haired, of the hero spake;

thick-haired, spoke of the hero;

the warrior would not, they weened, again,

the warrior would not, they believed,

proud of conquest, come to seek

proud of conquest, resurface to seek

their mighty master. To many it seemed

their mighty master. To many of them it seemed

the wolf-of-the-waves had won his life.

that Grendel's mother had taken his life.

The ninth hour came. The noble Scyldings

The ninth hour [since Beowulf's departure] came. The noble Scyldings

left the headland; homeward went

left the headland; returned home

the gold-friend of men. But the guests sat on,

that great friend of men [Hrothgar]. But the guests [Beowulf's men] sat on,

stared at the surges, sick in heart,

stared at the waves, sick in heart,

and wished, yet weened not, their winsome lord

and wished, yet did not believe, their lovable lord

again to see.
would return, and they would see him again.

Now that sword began
Now that sword started

from blood of the fight, in battle-droppings,
from the blood of the fight, the poisonous remains,

war-blade, to wane: 'twas a wondrous thing
the war-blade, to dissolve: it was an amazing thing

that all of it melted as ice is wont
that all of it melted as ice tends to do

when frosty fetters the Father loosens,
when our Heavenly Father melts the frost,

unwinds the wave-bonds, wielding all
releases the sea, controlling all

seasons and times: the true God he!
seasons and times: the true God he is!

Nor took from that dwelling the duke of the Geats
The duke of the Geats did not take from that den

save only the head and that hilt withal
the sword, except for the hilt and handle,

blazoned with jewels: the blade had melted,
embedded with jewels: the blade had melted,

burned was the bright sword, her blood was so hot,

her blood was so hot it destroyed the bright sword [like acid],

so poisoned the hell-sprite who perished within there.

so poisoned the hellish spirit who died in there.

Soon he was swimming who safe saw in combat

Soon he was swimming, the man who safely caused

downfall of demons; up-dove through the flood.

the downfall of demons; emerged from the waves.

The clashing waters were cleansed now,

The clashing waters had been made clean now,

waste of waves, where the wandering fiend

the empty lake, where the wandering fiend

her life-days left and this lapsing world.

left behind her life and this world.

Swam then to strand the sailors'-refuge,

He swam then to stand upon the shore,

sturdy-in-spirit, of sea-booty glad,

sturdy-in-spirit, glad to have found treasure,

of burden brave he bore with him.

the brave burden he brought with him.

Went then to greet him, and God they thanked,

They went then to greet him, thanking God,

the thane-band choice of their chieftain blithe,

the joyous thane-band to their chief,

that safe and sound they could see him again.

that they could see him again safe and sound.

Soon from the hardy one helmet and armor

Soon they took the helmet and armor

deftly they doffed: now drowsed the mere,

skillfully off him: now the lake was quiet,

water 'neath welkin, with war-blood stained.

water under the sky, stained with war-blood.

Forth they fared by the footpaths thence,

They went on by the footpaths from there,

merry at heart the highways measured,

travelled the highways while happy at heart,

well-known roads. Courageous men

the well-known roads. Courageous men

carried the head from the cliff by the sea,

carried the head from the cliff by the sea [back to Heorot]

an arduous task for all the band,

a difficult and tiring task for all the band,

the firm in fight, since four were needed
the loyal in battle, since four were needed

on the shaft-of-slaughter strenuously

to use all their strength to carry

to bear to the gold-hall Grendel's head.

Grendel's head to the gold-hall.

So presently to the palace there

They came eventually to the palace there

foemen fearless, fourteen Geats,

fourteen fearless Geats,

marching came. Their master-of-clan

marching along. Their master

mighty amid them the meadow-ways trod.

walked the meadow-ways mightily among them.

Strode then within the sovran thane

Inside then he strode, the sovereign thane

fearless in fight, of fame renowned,

fearless in fight, the famous,

hardy hero, Hrothgar to greet.

hardy hero, to greet Hrothgar.

And next by the hair into hall was borne

And next, into the hall, by the hair was carried

Grendel's head, where the henchmen were drinking,

Grendel's head, to where the henchmen were drinking.

an awe to clan and queen alike,

an amazing sight to both the clan and the queen,

a monster of marvel: the men looked on.
a marvelous monster: the men looked on.

~*~

Section XXIV

BEOWULF spake, bairn of Ecgtheow: --

BEOWULF spoke, the son of Ecgtheow: --

"Lo, now, this sea-booty, son of Healfdene,

"*See, now, this treasure from the sea, son of Healfdene,*

Lord of Scyldings, we've lustily brought thee,

Lord of Scyldings, we've eagerly brought you,

sign of glory; thou seest it here.

a sign of glory; you see it here.

Not lightly did I with my life escape!

I did not easily escape with my life!

In war under water this work I essayed

In war under water I did this work

with endless effort; and even so

with endless effort; and even with all that

my strength had been lost had the Lord not shielded me.

I would have lost my strength without God's protection.

Not a whit could I with Hrunting do

I could do nothing with Hrunting,

in work of war, though the weapon is good;

though the weapon is good;

yet a sword the Sovran of Men vouchsafed me

yet the Sovereign of Men provided me a sword

to spy on the wall there, in splendor hanging,

to spot on the wall there, hanging in splendor,

old, gigantic, -- how oft He guides

old, gigantic, -- of often He guides

the friendless wight! -- and I fought with that brand,

the friendless being! -- and I fought with that weapon,

felling in fight, since fate was with me,

felling in the fight, since fate favored me,

the house's wardens. That war-sword then

the house's monster. That war-sword then

all burned, bright blade, when the blood gushed o'er it,

all burned, the bright blade, when the blood gushed over it,

battle-sweat hot; but the hilt I brought back

the hot battle-sweat; but I brought back the hilt

from my foes. So avenged I their fiendish deeds

from my foes. In this way I avenged their fiendish deeds

death-fall of Danes, as was due and right.

the deaths of the Danes, as was right and proper.

And this is my hest, that in Heorot now

And this is my promise, that in Heorot now

safe thou canst sleep with thy soldier band,

you can sleep safely with your band of soldiers,

and every thane of all thy folk

and every thane of all your people

both old and young; no evil fear,

old and young; fear no evil

Scyldings' lord, from that side again,

Scyldings' lord, from that source again,

aught ill for thy earls, as erst thou must!"

will bad things come for your nobles, as you had to fear before!"

Then the golden hilt, for that gray-haired leader,

Then the golden [giant sword] hilt, for that gray-haired leader

hoary hero, in hand was laid,

the sturdy hero, was laid in his hand,

giant-wrought, old. So owned and enjoyed it

giant-made, old. So he owned and enjoyed its use

after downfall of devils, the Danish lord,

the Danish lord, after the downfall of devils,

wonder-smiths' work, since the world was rid

wonderful smith-work, since the world had been rid

of that grim-souled fiend, the foe of God,

if that terrible fiend, the enemy of God,

murder-marked, and his mother as well.

murderer, and his mother as well.

Now it passed into power of the people's king,

Now it belonged to the people's king,

best of all that the oceans bound

the best treasure of all the oceans

who have scattered their gold o'er Scandia's isle.
that have scattered their gold over the island of Scandia.

Hrothgar spake -- the hilt he viewed,

Hrothgar spoke -- he looked at the hilt,

heirloom old, where was etched the rise

the heirloom old, where was etched the course

of that far-off fight when the floods o'erwhelmed,

of that long-ago fight when the floods overwhelmed,

raging waves, the race of giants

those raging waves drowned the race of giants

(fearful their fate!), a folk estranged

(a terrible fate!), a people no longer governed

from God Eternal: whence guerdon due

by God Eternal: from that their punishment

in that waste of waters the Wielder paid them.

in that waste of waters God gave them.

So on the guard of shining gold

So on the hand-guard of shining gold

in runic staves it was rightly said

in ancient runes it correctly said

for whom the serpent-traced sword was wrought,

for whom the serpent-decorated sword was made,

best of blades, in bygone days,

best of blades, in days gone by,

and the hilt well wound. -- The wise-one spake,

and the hilt well wound. -- The wise one spoke,

son of Healfdene; silent were all: --

the son of Healfdene; all were silent: --

"Lo, so may he say who sooth and right

"Indeed, he may say who truth and right

follows 'mid folk, of far times mindful,

follows among the people, thinking of the future,

a land-warden old, that this earl belongs

an old ruler, that this earl belongs

to the better breed! So, borne aloft,

to the better breed! So, carried above,

thy fame must fly, O friend my Beowulf,

your fame must fly, O Beowulf my friend,

far and wide o'er folksteads many. Firmly thou

far and wide over many towns. You firmly

shalt all maintain,

shall maintain,

mighty strength with mood of wisdom. Love of mine will I assure thee,

mighty strength together with wisdom. My love I will reaffirm for you,

as, awhile ago, I promised; thou shalt prove a stay

as, a while ago, I promised: you shall prove a blessing

in future, in far-off years, to folk of thine,

in the future, years from now, to your people,

to the heroes a help. Was not Heremod thus

a help to heroes. Heremod was not like this

to offspring of Ecgwela, Honor-Scyldings,

to the children of Ecgwela, of the Honor-Scyldings

nor grew for their grace, but for grisly slaughter,

not destined for peace, but for grisly slaughter,

for doom of death to the Danishmen.
for doom of death to the Danish.

He slew, wrath-swollen, his shoulder-comrades,

He killed, filled with wrath, his own comrades,

companions at board! So he passed alone,

companions and allies! So he passed alone,

chieftain haughty, from human cheer.

the vain chief, from human company.

Though him the Maker with might endowed,

Though God had given him great strength.

delights of power, and uplifted high

delights of power, and lifted him high

above all men, yet blood-fierce his mind,

above all men, yet his mind was fierce,

his breast-hoard, grew, no bracelets gave he

his selfish treasure hoard grew, no bracelets gave he

to Danes as was due; he endured all joyless

to Danes as he should have; he endured all unhappy

strain of struggle and stress of woe,

the strain of struggle and stress of sorrow,

long feud with his folk. Here find thy lesson!

long feud with his folk. Learn a lesson from him!

Of virtue advise thee! This verse I have said for thee,

Let it advise you about virtue! This poem I have quoted for you,

wise from lapsed winters. Wondrous seems

wise from my many years. It seems amazing

how to sons of men Almighty God

how to human beings Almighty God

in the strength of His spirit sendeth wisdom,

sends wisdom in the strength of His spirit,

estate, high station: He swayeth all things.

ownership, high station: He controls all things.

Whiles He letteth right lustily fare

When he allows for goodness to eagerly push

the heart of the hero of high-born race, --

the heart of the highly-born hero, --

in seat ancestral assigns him bliss,

gives him an ancestral throne and grants him bliss,,

his folk's sure fortress in fee to hold,

to be responsible for his people's fortress,

puts in his power great parts of the earth,

puts vast portions of the earth in his power,

empire so ample, that end of it

an empire so generous, that the end of it

this wanter-of-wisdom weeneth none.

even a seeker of wisdom cannot imagine.

So he waxes in wealth, nowise can harm him

So he grows in wealth, nothing can harm him

illness or age; no evil cares

illness or age; no great worries

shadow his spirit; no sword-hate threatens

shadow his spirit; no violence threatens

from ever an enemy: all the world

from any enemy ever: all the world

wends at his will, no worse he knoweth,

goes according to his plans, he knows nothing bad

till all within him obstinate pride

until all within him stubborn pride

waxes and wakes while the warden slumbers,

grows and wakes when the guardian sleeps,

the spirit's sentry; sleep is too fast

the spirit's sentry; sleep is too sound

which masters his might, and the murderer nears,

which controls his power, and the murderer comes near,

stealthily shooting the shafts from his bow!

stealthily shooting arrows from his bow!

~*~

Section XXV

"UNDER harness his heart then is hit indeed

"UNDER his armor his hart was then hit

by sharpest shafts; and no shelter avails

by the sharpest arrows; and no shelter can protect him

from foul behest of the hellish fiend.

from the terrible plans of the hellish fiend [the Devil].

Him seems too little what long he possessed.

His possessions he has had so long seems to little.

Greedy and grim, no golden rings

Greedy and grim, he gives no rings

he gives for his pride; the promised future

away in his pride; the promised future

forgets he and spurns, with all God has sent him,

he forgets and rejects, with all God has sent him,

Wonder-Wielder, of wealth and fame.

God of Wonder, all the wealth and fame.

Yet in the end it ever comes

Yet in the end it always comes

that the frame of the body fragile yields,

that the fragile body gives up,

fated falls; and there follows another

death comes as fated; and someone else comes

who joyously the jewels divides,

who joyously shares the jewels,

the royal riches, nor recks of his forebear.

the royal riches, not thinking of his predecessor.

Ban, then, such baleful thoughts, Beowulf dearest,

Keep from you mind, then, such bad thoughts, dearest Beowulf,

best of men, and the better part choose,

best of men, and choose the better part,

profit eternal; and temper thy pride,

eternal profit; and hold back your pride

warrior famous! The flower of thy might

famous warrior! The peak of your power

lasts now a while: but erelong it shall be

will last for a while: but in not too long it shall happen

that sickness or sword thy strength shall minish,

that through sickness or injury your strength will diminish,

or fang of fire, or flooding billow,

or flames of fire, or washing waves,

or bite of blade, or brandished spear,

or slash of sword, or brandished spear,

or odious age; or the eyes' clear beam

or terrible old age; or the clear vision of your eyes

wax dull and darken: Death even thee

go dull and dark: even you, when Death comes

in haste shall o'erwhelm, thou hero of war!

shall be quickly overwhelmed, you hero of war!

So the Ring-Danes these half-years a hundred I ruled,

So I have ruled these Ring-Danes for fifty years,

wielded 'neath welkin, and warded them bravely

beneath the sky, and protected them bravely

from mighty-ones many o'er middle-earth,

from many mighty ones over the earth,

from spear and sword, till it seemed for me

from spears and swords, until it seemed to me

no foe could be found under fold of the sky.

that no foe could no longer be found.

Lo, sudden the shift! To me seated secure

Then, the sudden change! To my secure seat

came grief for joy when Grendel began

grief replaced joy when Grendel began

to harry my home, the hellish foe;

to trouble my home, the hellish foe;

for those ruthless raids, unresting I suffered

for those ruthless raids, I suffered without resting,

heart-sorrow heavy. Heaven be thanked,

my heart heavy with sorrow. Heaven be thanked,

Lord Eternal, for life extended

to eternal God, for my renewed life

that I on this head all hewn and bloody,

that I may look upon this head all chopped and bloody,

after long evil, with eyes may gaze!

my eyes gaze on it after long evil!

-- Go to the bench now! Be glad at banquet,

-- Go sit down now! Enjoy the banquet,

warrior worthy! A wealth of treasure at dawn of day, be dealt between us!"

worthy warrior! At dawn I will give you a wealth of treasure!"

Glad was the Geats' lord, going betimes

The Geats' lord was glad, going then

to seek his seat, as the Sage commanded.
to take his seat, as the Wise One commanded.

Afresh, as before, for the famed-in-battle,
Freshly made, as before, for the famed-in-battle,

for the band of the hall, was a banquet dight
for the crowd in the hall, was a banquet prepared

nobly anew. The Night-Helm darkened
nobly anew. The night sky darkened

dusk o'er the drinkers.
dusk over the drinkers.

The doughty ones rose:
The courageous ones rose:

for the hoary-headed would hasten to rest,
for the solid-headed would hurry to rest,

aged Scylding; and eager the Geat,
the aged Scylding; and the Geat was eager,

shield-fighter sturdy, for sleeping yearned.
the sturdy shield-fighter longed for sleep.

Him wander-weary, warrior-guest

Tired from wandering, the warrior guest

from far, a hall-thane heralded forth,

from far, a servant came forth,

who by custom courtly cared for all

who customarily took care of all

needs of a thane as in those old days

the needs of a man as in those old days

warrior-wanderers wont to have.

wandering warriors tended to have.

So slumbered the stout-heart. Stately the hall

So the stout-heart slept. The stately hall

rose gabled and gilt where the guest slept on

rose gabled and covered in gold where the guest slept on

till a raven black the rapture-of-heaven

until a black raven

blithe-heart boded. Bright came flying

brought good luck and happiness. Brightly came flying

shine after shadow. The swordsmen hastened,

shine after shadow. The swordsmen rushed,

athelings all were eager homeward

warriors all were eager to return home,

forth to fare; and far from thence

and far from there

the great-hearted guest would guide his keel.

the great-hearted guest would steer his ship.

Bade then the hardy-one Hrunting be brought

Beowulf commanded that the sword Hrunting be brought

to the son of Ecglaf, the sword bade him take,

to the son of Ecglaf (Unferth), telling him to take it back,

excellent iron, and uttered his thanks for it,

the excellent iron, and thanked him for it,

quoth that he counted it keen in battle,

saying that he found it helpful in battle,

"war-friend" winsome: with words he slandered not

a friend in war: he did not mention the failure

edge of the blade: 'twas a big-hearted man!

of the blade's edge: he was a big-hearted man!

Now eager for parting and armed at point

Now eager for departure and armed properly

180

warriors waited, while went to his host

the warriors waited, while went to his host

that Darling of Danes. The doughty atheling

that Darling of Danes. The brave warrior

to high-seat hastened and Hrothgar greeted.

hurried to the throne and greeted Hrothgar.

~*~

Section XXVI

BEOWULF spake, bairn of Ecgtheow: --

BEOWULF spoke, the son of Ecgtheow: --

"Lo, we seafarers say our will,

"See, we sea travelers say our desire,

far-come men, that we fain would seek

men from far away, that we plan to go

Hygelac now. We here have found

back to Hygelac now. Here we have found

hosts to our heart: thou hast harbored us well.

hosts after our own hearts: you have cared for us well

If ever on earth I am able to win me

If I am ever able to gain myself

more of thy love, O lord of men,

more of your love, Oh lord of men,

aught anew, than I now have done,

all over again, the things I have done,

for work of war I am willing still!

in the name of war, I am willing still!

If it come to me ever across the seas

If news ever comes to me across the seas

that neighbor foemen annoy and fright thee, --
that neighboring enemies annoy and frighten you, --

as they that hate thee erewhile have used, --
as they that hate you have used before, --
thousands then of thanes I shall bring,
I shall bring thousands of men,

heroes to help thee. Of Hygelac I know,
heroes to help you. I know of Hygelac,

ward of his folk, that, though few his years,
ruler of his people, that, though he is young,

the lord of the Geats will give me aid
the lord of the Geats will give me help

by word and by work, that well I may serve thee,
by word and by action, that I may serve you well,

wielding the war-wood to win thy triumph
using the war-spear to win your triumph

and lending thee might when thou lackest men.
and lending you power when you lack in men.

If thy Hrethric should come to court of Geats,

If your Hrethric should come to the court of the Geats,

a sovran's son, he will surely there

a sovereign's son, he will surely

find his friends. A far-off land

find friends there. A far-off land

each man should visit who vaunts him brave."

every man should visit who considers himself brave."

Him then answering, Hrothgar spake: --

Answering then, Hrothgar spoke: --

"These words of thine the wisest God

"These words of yours the wisest God

sent to thy soul! No sager counsel

sent to your soul! No wiser advice

from so young in years e'er yet have I heard.

from someone so young I have ever heard before,

Thou art strong of main and in mind art wary,

You are strong of body and in mind as well,

art wise in words! I ween indeed

are wise in words! I believe indeed

if ever it hap that Hrethel's heir

if ever it happens that Hrethel's heir

by spear be seized, by sword-grim battle,

is stabbed by the spear, in sword-grim battle,

by illness or iron, thine elder and lord,

by illness or weapon, your elder and lord,

people's leader, -- and life be thine, --

the people's leader, -- and you are still alive, --

no seemlier man will the Sea-Geats find

no better man would the Sea-Geats find

at all to choose for their chief and king,

to choose for their chief and king, at all,

for hoard-guard of heroes, if hold thou wilt

for the guardian of heroes, if you will hold

thy kinsman's kingdom! Thy keen mind pleases me

your kinsman's kingdom! Your sharp mind pleases me

the longer the better, Beowulf loved!

and may you live long, beloved Beowulf!

Thou hast brought it about that both our peoples,

You have made it happen that both our peoples,

sons of the Geat and Spear-Dane folk,

both the Geats and Danes,

shall have mutual peace, and from murderous strife,

shall have mutual peace, and from murderous conflict,

such as once they waged, from war refrain.

such as they once waged, they will refrain.

Long as I rule this realm so wide,

As long as I rule this wide realm,

let our hoards be common, let heroes with gold

let our hoards be shared, let heroes with gold

each other greet o'er the gannet's-bath,

greet each other over the ocean

and the ringed-prow bear o'er rolling waves

and the ships carry over rolling waves

tokens of love. I trow my landfolk

tokens of respect. I swear that my people

towards friend and foe are firmly joined,

are firmly joined towards friend and foe,

and honor they keep in the olden way."

and keep honor in the traditional way."

To him in the hall, then, Healfdene's son

To him [Beowulf] in the hall, then, Healfdene's son

gave treasures twelve, and the trust-of-earls

gave him twelve treasures, and the king

bade him fare with the gifts to his folk beloved,

told him to return with the gifts to his beloved folk,

hale to his home, and in haste return.

healthy to his home, and return soon.

Then kissed the king of kin renowned,

Then Hrothgar kissed,

Scyldings' chieftain, that choicest thane,

chief of Scyldings, that best of men,

and fell on his neck. Fast flowed the tears

and embraced him. His tears flowed fast.

of the hoary-headed. Heavy with winters,

Old in years,

he had chances twain, but he clung to this, --

he had had two chances, but he clung to this hope, -

that each should look on the other again,

that they would see each other again,

and hear him in hall. Was this hero so dear to him,

and hear Beowulf again in the hall. This hero was so dear to him

his breast's wild billows he banned in vain;

his chest's wild beating he tried to stop in vain;

safe in his soul a secret longing,

safe in his soul a secret wanting ,

locked in his mind, for that loved man

locked in his mind, for that beloved man

burned in his blood. Then Beowulf strode,

burning in his blood. Then Beowulf walked,

glad of his gold-gifts, the grass-plot o'er,

glad of his golden gifts, over the grass-plot,

warrior blithe. The wave-roamer bode

a carefree warrior. The sea-ship stayed

riding at anchor, its owner awaiting.

floating at anchor, its owner waiting.

As they hastened onward, Hrothgar's gift

As they hurried onward, Hrothgar's gift

they lauded at length. -- 'Twas a lord unpeered,

they praised for a long time. – He was a matchless ruler,

every way blameless, till age had broken

in every way virtuous, until age had broken

-- it spareth no mortal -- his splendid might.

-- it spares no mortal – his splendid power.

~*~

Section XXVII

CAME now to ocean the ever-courageous

THEY CAME now to the ocean, the ever-courageous

hardy henchmen, their harness bearing,

hardy henchmen, carrying their gear,

woven war-sarks. The warden marked,

woven war flags. The guard observed,

trusty as ever, the earl's return.

trustworthy as ever, the noble's return.

From the height of the hill no hostile words

From the top of the hill no hostile words

reached the guests as he rode to greet them;

reached the guests [to Heorot] as he rode to greet them;

but "Welcome!" he called to that Weder clan

but "Welcome!" he called to that group of Weders

as the sheen-mailed spoilers to ship marched on.

as the shiny-with-chain-mail soldiers marched on to the ship.

Then on the strand, with steeds and treasure

Then on the shore, with horses and treasure

and armor their roomy and ring-dight ship

and armor their roomy and ring-decked ship

was heavily laden: high its mast

was heavily loaded: its high mast

rose over Hrothgar's hoarded gems.

rose over Hrothgar's collected gems.

A sword to the boat-guard Beowulf gave,

Beowulf gave a sword to the boat-guard,

mounted with gold; on the mead-bench since

one plated with gold;on the mead-bench since

he was better esteemed, that blade possessing,

he would be more admired if he had that blade,

heirloom old. -- Their ocean-keel boarding,

the old heirloom. -- Boarding their ship,

they drove through the deep, and Daneland left.

they sailed through the deep, and left Denmark.

A sea-cloth was set, a sail with ropes,

They set the sea-cloth, a sail with ropes,

firm to the mast; the flood-timbers moaned;

firmly to the mast; the planks creaked;

nor did wind over billows that wave-swimmer blow

but the wind over the waves did not blow that ship

across from her course. The craft sped on,

off her course. The craft sped on,

foam-necked it floated forth o'er the waves,

it floated foamy forth over the waves,

keel firm-bound over briny currents,

its keel firmly bound over the salty currents,

till they got them sight of the Geatish cliffs,

until they were within sight of the Geatish cliffs,

home-known headlands. High the boat,

their well-known home headlands. The boat

stirred by winds, on the strand updrove.

stirred by wins, drove high onto the shore.

Helpful at haven the harbor-guard stood,

The harbor-guard stood, ready to help,

who long already for loved companions

who had already, for a long time waited

by the water had waited and watched afar.

for his beloved companions and watched afar.

He bound to the beach the broad-bosomed ship
He bound to the beach that broad ship

with anchor-bands, lest ocean-billows
with anchors, so that ocean waves

that trusty timber should tear away.
would not tear away that trusty timber.

Then Beowulf bade them bear the treasure,
Then Bewoful told them to take the treasure,

gold and jewels; no journey far
gold and jewels; it was not a far journey

was it thence to go to the giver of rings,
from there to go to the king,

Hygelac Hrethling: at home he dwelt
Hegelac Hrethling: he lived at home

by the sea-wall close, himself and clan.
close to the seashore, himself and his clan.

Haughty that house, a hero the king,
The house was proud, the king a hero,

high the hall, and Hygd right young,

the hall was tall, and Hygd (the Queen) youthful,

wise and wary, though winters few

wise and clever, despite being so young

in those fortress walls she had found a home,

in those fortress walls she had made herself a home,

Haereth's daughter. Nor humble her ways,

Haereth's daughter. Her ways were not lowly,

nor grudged she gifts to the Geatish men,

and she was generous in giving gifts to the Geatish men,

of precious treasure. Not Thryth's pride showed she,

of precious treasure. She showed no excessive pride, either,

folk-queen famed, or that fell deceit.

that famous folk-queen, or evil lies.

Was none so daring that durst make bold

There were none so brave that dared

(save her lord alone) of the liegemen dear

(except for her father) of the dear nobleman

that lady full in the face to look,

to look that lady fully in the face,

but forged fetters he found his lot,

but in chains he found himself,

bonds of death! And brief the respite;

the bonds of death! And the break was short;

soon as they seized him, his sword-doom was spoken,

as soon as they seized him, his execution was planned,

and the burnished blade a baleful murder

and the polished sword a terrible murder

proclaimed and closed. No queenly way

commanded and carried out. This was no queenly way

for woman to practise, though peerless she,

for a woman to behave, though she was without match,

that the weaver-of-peace from warrior dear

that a dear and good warrior

by wrath and lying his life should reave!

should lose his life because of such anger!

But Hemming's kinsman hindered this. –

But Hemming's kinsman put a stop to this. –

For over their ale men also told

For over their drinks men also told

that of these folk-horrors fewer she wrought,
that of these horrors she did far fewer,

onslaughts of evil, after she went,
such actions of evil, after she went,

gold-decked bride, to the brave young prince,
gold-covered bride, to the brave young prince,

atheling haughty, and Offa's hall
proud warrior, and Offa's hall

o'er the fallow flood at her father's bidding
over the water at her father's command

safely sought, where since she prospered,
safely brought, where since she prospered,

royal, throned, rich in goods,
royal, with a throne, rich in goods,

fain of the fair life fate had sent her,
pleased with the lovely life fate had sent her,

and leal in love to the lord of warriors.
and deeply in love with the lord of warriors.

He, of all heroes I heard of ever

He, of all the heroes I have ever heard of

from sea to sea, of the sons of earth,

from sea to sea, of the children of men,

most excellent seemed. Hence Offa was praised

seemed most excellent. So Offa was praised

for his fighting and feeing by far-off men,

for his fighting and generosity by far-off men

the spear-bold warrior; wisely he ruled

the bold warrior; he ruled wisely

over his empire. Eomer woke to him,

over his empire. Eomer was born to him,

help of heroes, Hemming's kinsman,

the help of heroes, Hemming's kinsman,

Grandson of Garmund, grim in war.

The grandson of Garmund, grim in war.

~*~

Section XXVIII

HASTENED the hardy one, henchmen with him,

THE HARDY one hurried, his henchmen with him,

sandy strand of the sea to tread

to walk the sandy shore of the sea

and widespread ways. The world's great candle,

and widely spread ways. The world's great candle,

sun shone from south. They strode along

the sun shone from the south. They walked along

with sturdy steps to the spot they knew

with sturdy steps to the place they knew

where the battle-king young, his burg within,

where the young battle-king, his city inside,

slayer of Ongentheow, shared the rings,

killer of Ongentheow, shared his wealth,

shelter-of-heroes. To Hygelac

the shelter-of-heroes. To Hygelac

Beowulf's coming was quickly told, --

Beowulf's arrival was quickly told, --

that there in the court the clansmen's refuge,

that there in the court the protector of clansmen,

the shield-companion sound and alive,

the shield-companion was safe and sound,

hale from the hero-play homeward strode.

walking home healthy from heroics.

With haste in the hall, by highest order,

Hurrying in the hall, by highest order,

room for the rovers was readily made.

room was quickly made for the rovers.

By his sovran he sat, come safe from battle,

By his sovereign he sat, returned safe from battle,

kinsman by kinsman. His kindly lord

kinsman by kinsman. His kind lord

he first had greeted in gracious form,

he had first greeted graciously,

with manly words. The mead dispensing,

with manly words. Sharing the mead,

came through the high hall Haereth's daughter,

Haereth's daughter came through the high hall,

winsome to warriors, wine-cup bore

appealing to warriors, carrying the wine-cup

to the hands of the heroes. Hygelac then

to the hands of the heroes. [King] Hygelac then

his comrade fairly with question plied

asked many questions of his comrade

in the lofty hall, sore longing to know

in the lofty hall, intensely wanting to know

what manner of sojourn the Sea-Geats made.

what king of journey the Geats had made over the sea.

"What came of thy quest, my kinsman Beowulf,

"What came of your quest, my kinsman Beowfulf,

when thy yearnings suddenly swept thee yonder

when your desires suddenly swept you there

battle to seek o'er the briny sea,

to look for a fight over the salty sea,

combat in Heorot? Hrothgar couldst thou

combat in Heorot? Were you able to

aid at all, the honored chief,

help Hrothgar, the honored chief,

in his wide-known woes? With waves of care

in his widely-known troubles? With waves of worry

my sad heart seethed; I sore mistrusted

my sad heart seethed; I deeply distrusted

my loved one's venture: long I begged thee

my loved one's adventure: I begged you for ages

by no means to seek that slaughtering monster,

to by no means search for that slaughtering monster,

but suffer the South-Danes to settle their feud

but allow the South-Danes to settle their feud

themselves with Grendel. Now God be thanked

with Grendel by themselves. Now God be thanked

that safe and sound I can see thee now!"

that I can see you now safe and sound!"

Beowulf spake, the bairn of Ecgtheow: --

Beowulf spoke, the son of Ecgtheow: --

"'Tis known and unhidden, Hygelac Lord,

"It is known and not a secret, Lord Hygelac,

to many men, that meeting of ours,

to many men, that fight of ours,

struggle grim between Grendel and me,

the grim struggle between Grendel and me,

which we fought on the field where full too many

which we fought in the hall where far to many

sorrows he wrought for the Scylding-Victors,

sorrows he brought upon the Scyldings,

evils unending. These all I avenged.

unending evils. I avenged all these.

No boast can be from breed of Grendel,

No bragging can come from Grendel's people

any on earth, for that uproar at dawn,

any still alive, for that uproar at dawn,

from the longest-lived of the loathsome race

from the longest-lived of that loathsome kind

in fleshly fold! -- But first I went

in this life! – But first I went

Hrothgar to greet in the hall of gifts,

to greet Hrothgar in the hall of gifts,

where Healfdene's kinsman high-renowned,

where Healfene's highly renowned kinsman;

soon as my purpose was plain to him,

as soon as my purpose was clear to him,

assigned me a seat by his son and heir.

gave me a [honored] seat by his son and heir.

The liegemen were lusty; my life-days never

The liegemen were eager; in all my life never

such merry men over mead in hall

such merry men over mean in a hall

have I heard under heaven! The high-born queen,

have I ever heard! The high-born queen,

people's peace-bringer, passed through the hall,

bringer of peace, came through the hall,

cheered the young clansmen, clasps of gold,

bringing cheer to the young clansmen, gold clasps,

ere she sought her seat, to sundry gave.

she gave to various of them, before she went to her seat.

Oft to the heroes Hrothgar's daughter,

Often to the heroes Hrothgar's daughter,

to earls in turn, the ale-cup tendered, --

brought the ale-cup to nobles in turn, --

she whom I heard these hall-companions

the woman whom I heard these companions

Freawaru name, when fretted gold

call Freawaru, when finely worked gold

she proffered the warriors. Promised is she,

she offered to the warriors. She is betrothed,

gold-decked maid, to the glad son of Froda.

the gold-decked maid, to the pleased son of Froda.

Sage this seems to the Scylding's-friend,

He seems wise, this Scylding's-friend,

kingdom's-keeper: he counts it wise

keeper of the kingdom: he thinks it wise

the woman to wed so and ward off feud,

to do such matchmaking and prevent war

store of slaughter. But seldom ever

and useless slaughter. But it is rare

when men are slain, does the murder-spear sink

when men are killed, that the murder-spear sinks

204

but briefest while, though the bride be fair!

more than the shortest time, though the bride is beautiful!

"Nor haply will like it the Heathobard lord,

"Not greatly will the Heathobard lord like it,

and as little each of his liegemen all,

and all his liegeman will like it even less,

when a thane of the Danes, in that doughty throng,

when a thane of the Danes, in that tough throng,

goes with the lady along their hall,

goes with the lady down their hall,

and on him the old-time heirlooms glisten

and on him the ancient heirlooms glisten

hard and ring-decked, Heathobard's treasure,

hard and ring-covered, Heathobard's treasure,

weapons that once they wielded fair

weapons that once they wielded well

until they lost at the linden-play

until they lost in battle

liegeman leal and their lives as well.

the loyalty of liegemen and their lives as well.

Then, over the ale, on this heirloom gazing,

And then, over his ale, gazing on this heirloom,

some ash-wielder old who has all in mind

some old spear-warrior who remembers

that spear-death of men, -- he is stern of mood,

that spear-death of men, -- he is gloomy in mood,

heavy at heart, -- in the hero young

heavy at heart, -- and in the young hero

tests the temper and tries the soul

it tests the temper and stresses the soul

and war-hate wakens, with words like these: --

and war-hate returns, with words like these: --

Canst thou not, comrade, ken that sword

Can you not, comrade, remember that sword

which to the fray thy father carried

which to the fight your father carried

in his final feud, 'neath the fighting-mask,

in his final feud, beneath the helmet,

dearest of blades, when the Danish slew him

most precious of blades, when the Danish killed him

and wielded the war-place on Withergild's fall,
and fought with the sword on Withergild's fall,

after havoc of heroes, those hardy Scyldings?
after the havoc of heroes, those hardy Scyldings?

Now, the son of a certain slaughtering Dane,
Now, the son of a certain killing Dane,

proud of his treasure, paces this hall,
proud of his treasure, walks this hall,

joys in the killing, and carries the jewel
takes joy in the killing, and carries the jewel

that rightfully ought to be owned by thee!
that rightfully ought to be yours!

Thus he urges and eggs him all the time
In this way he urges and pushes him all the time

with keenest words, till occasion offers
with eager words, until the chance comes

that Freawaru's thane, for his father's deed,
that Freawaru's man, for his father's action

,

after bite of brand in his blood must slumber,

after the stab of a sword must die,

losing his life; but that liegeman flies
losing his life; but that liegeman escapes

living away, for the land he kens.
living away, for the land he knows.

And thus be broken on both their sides
"And in this way it is broken on both sides

oaths of the earls, when Ingeld's breast
the oaths of the nobles, when Ingeld's heart

wells with war-hate, and wife-love now
wells with war-hate, and the love of his wife

after the care-billows cooler grows.
after the storms of worry grows cooler.

"So I hold not high the Heathobards' faith
"So I do not think much of the Heathobard's faith

due to the Danes, or their during love
due to the Danes, or their enduring love

and pact of peace. -- But I pass from that,
and peace treaty. – But I will move on from that,

turning to Grendel, O giver-of-treasure,

and return to Grendel, Oh giver-of-treasure,

and saying in full how the fight resulted,

and explain fully how the fight ended up,

hand-fray of heroes. When heaven's jewel

the hand-to-hand combat of heroes. When the sun

had fled o'er far fields, that fierce sprite came,

had set over the far fields, that fierce spirit came,

night-foe savage, to seek us out

savage night-foe, to find us

where safe and sound we sentried the hall.

where we guarded the hall safe and sound.

To Hondscio then was that harassing deadly,

The attack was deadly to Hondscio then,

his fall there was fated. He first was slain,

his fall there was fated. He was killed first,

girded warrior. Grendel on him

the armored warrior. Grendel on him

turned murderous mouth, on our mighty kinsman,

turned his horrible hunger, on our mighty kinsman,

and all of the brave man's body devoured.

and devoured all of the brave man's body.

Yet none the earlier, empty-handed,

Yet he would not immediately, empty handed,

would the bloody-toothed murderer, mindful of bale,

with evil on his mind would the bloody-toothed murderer

outward go from the gold-decked hall:

leave the gold-decorated hall:

but me he attacked in his terror of might,

but he attacked me in his terrible might,

with greedy hand grasped me. A glove hung by him

and grasped me with a greedy hand. A glove hung by him

wide and wondrous, wound with bands;

big and amazing, with bands wound around it;

and in artful wise it all was wrought,

and in great skill it was wrought,

by devilish craft, of dragon-skins.

devilishly crafted out of dragon skins.

Me therein, an innocent man,

Me inside, an innocent man,

the fiendish foe was fain to thrust

the fiendish foe decided to fight

with many another. He might not so,

with many another. So that he could not,

when I all angrily upright stood.

I angrily stood upright.

'Twere long to relate how that land-destroyer

It would take ages to tell how that land-destroyer

I paid in kind for his cruel deeds;

I paid back for his cruel deeds;

yet there, my prince, this people of thine

yet there, my prince, this people of yours

got fame by my fighting. He fled away,

became famous through my fighting. He escaped,

and a little space his life preserved;

and preserved a little bit of his life;

but there staid behind him his stronger hand

but there stayed behind him his stronger hand

left in Heorot; heartsick thence

left in Heorot; in great pain from there

on the floor of the ocean that outcast fell.

that outcast sank to the floor of the ocean.

Me for this struggle the Scyldings'-friend

The Scyldings'-friend paid me for this struggle

paid in plenty with plates of gold,

in plenty with plates of gold,

with many a treasure, when morn had come

with many treasures, when the morning came

and we all at the banquet-board sat down.

and we all sat down at the banquet table.

Then was song and glee. The gray-haired Scylding,

Then there was song and celebration. The gray-haired Scylding

much tested, told of the times of yore.

who had endured much, told of the olden days.

Whiles the hero his harp bestirred,

While the hero played his harp,

wood-of-delight; now lays he chanted

that delightful wood; then he chanted epic poems

of sooth and sadness, or said aright

of truth and sadness, or plainly told

legends of wonder, the wide-hearted king;
wonderful legends, the big-hearted king;

or for years of his youth he would yearn at times,
or for the years of his youth he would long for at times,

for strength of old struggles, now stricken with age,
for the strength of his old struggles, now he was old,

hoary hero: his heart surged full
the solid hero: his heart was full

when, wise with winters, he wailed their flight.
when, wise with age, he mourned their passing.

Thus in the hall the whole of that day
In this way in the hall, all that day

at ease we feasted, till fell o'er earth
we feasted comfortably, until another night

another night. Anon full ready
fell over the earth. Now full ready

in greed of vengeance, Grendel's mother
in greed of revenge, Grendel's mother

set forth all doleful. Dead was her son

went forth all sadly. Her son was dead

through war-hate of Weders; now, woman monstrous

through the hate of Weders; now, the monstrous woman

with fury fell a foeman she slew,

killed a foe with fury,

avenged her offspring. From Aeschere old,

avenging her offspring. From old Aeschere,

loyal councillor, life was gone;

loyal counselor, life was gone;

nor might they e'en, when morning broke,

and they could not even, when morning came,

those Danish people, their death-done comrade

those Danish people, their murdered comrade

burn with brands, on balefire lay

respectfully cremate, lay on a bonfire

the man they mourned. Under mountain stream

the body of the man they mourned. Under a mountain stream

she had carried the corpse with cruel hands.

she had carried the corpse away with her cruel hands.

For Hrothgar that was the heaviest sorrow

For Hrothgar that was the worst sorrow

of all that had laden the lord of his folk.

of all that had burdened the lord of his people.

The leader then, by thy life, besought me

The leader then, by your life, begged me

(sad was his soul) in the sea-waves' coil

(his soul was sad) at the bottom of the sea

to play the hero and hazard my being

to play the hero and risk my life

for glory of prowess: my guerdon he pledged.

for the glory of skill: he promised my reward.

I then in the waters -- 'tis widely known –

I then in the waters – it is widely known –

that sea-floor-guardian savage found.

found that savage sea-floor guardian.

Hand-to-hand there a while we struggled;

We struggled hand-to-hand for a while;

billows welled blood; in the briny hall

the waves filling with blood; in the salty hall

her head I hewed with a hardy blade

I cut off her head with a hardy blade

from Grendel's mother, -- and gained my life,

from Grendel's mother's body, -- and saved my life,

though not without danger. My doom was not yet.

though not without danger. My time to die was not yet.

Then the haven-of-heroes, Healfdene's son,

Then the protector of heroes, Healfdene's son,

gave me in guerdon great gifts of price.

gave me, as promised, great and expensive gifts.

~*~

Section XXIX

"So held this king to the customs old,

"The king was so devoted to the old customs,

that I wanted for nought in the wage I gained,

that I lacked nothing in the payment I gained,

the meed of my might; he made me gifts,

the reward for my strength; he gave me gifts,

Healfdene's heir, for my own disposal.

Healfdene's heir, for my own use.

Now to thee, my prince, I proffer them all,

Now to you, my prince, I offer them all,

gladly give them. Thy grace alone

gladly give them. Your generosity alone

can find me favor. Few indeed

can fulfill my wishes. Few indeed

have I of kinsmen, save, Hygelac, thee!"

have I of family, except, Hygelac, you!"

Then he bade them bear him the boar-head standard,

Then he told his men to bring him the boar-head flag,

the battle-helm high, and breastplate gray,

the helmet high, and the gray breastplate,

the splendid sword; then spake in form: --

the splendid sword; then spoke formally: --

"Me this war-gear the wise old prince,

"This war gear the wise old prince,

Hrothgar, gave, and his hest he added,

Hrothgar, gave me, and asked also

that its story be straightway said to thee. --

that its story be told to you immediately. --

A while it was held by Heorogar king,

It belonged for a while to king Heorogar,

for long time lord of the land of Scyldings;

for a long time the ruler of the Scyldings;

yet not to his son the sovran left it,

yet the sovereign did not leave it to his son,

to daring Heoroweard, -- dear as he was to him,

to daring Heoroweard, -- beloved as he was to him,

his harness of battle. -- Well hold thou it all!"

his battle-armor. -- Hold it all well!"

And I heard that soon passed o'er the path of this treasure,

And I heard that soon passed over the path of this treasure,

all apple-fallow, four good steeds,

all full of apples, four good horses,

each like the others, arms and horses

each like the others, the weapons and horses

he gave to the king. So should kinsmen be,

he gave to the king. Kinsmen should be like that,

not weave one another the net of wiles,

not wrapping each other in a net of tricks,

or with deep-hid treachery death contrive

or with deeply hid treachery try to bring death

for neighbor and comrade. His nephew was ever

to neighbors and comrades. His nephew was always

by hardy Hygelac held full dear,

loved deeply by hardy Hygelac,

and each kept watch o'er the other's weal.

and they looked out for each other's welfare.

I heard, too, the necklace to Hygd he presented,

I heard, too, that he presented the necklace to Hygd,

wonder-wrought treasure, which Wealhtheow gave him

the wonderfully made treasure, which Wealhtheow gave him

sovran's daughter: three steeds he added,

the sovereigns daughter: three horses he added,

slender and saddle-gay. Since such gift

slender and energetic in their saddles. Since that gifting

the gem gleamed bright on the breast of the queen.

the gem has gleamed bright on the breast of the queen.

Thus showed his strain the son of Ecgtheow

In this way the son of Ecgtheow showed his nature

as a man remarked for mighty deeds

as a man known for mighty deeds

and acts of honor. At ale he slew not

and acts of honor. He never drunkenly killed

comrade or kin; nor cruel his mood,

comrade or kin; his mood was never cruel,

though of sons of earth his strength was greatest,

though his strength was the greatest of any man,

a glorious gift that God had sent

a glorious blessing that God had given

the splendid leader. Long was he spurned,

the splendid leader. For a long time he had been rejected,

and worthless by Geatish warriors held;

and considered worthless by Geatish warriors;

him at mead the master-of-clans

the master-at clans at mead

failed full oft to favor at all.

often failed to favor him at all.

Slack and shiftless the strong men deemed him,

The strong men thought him weak and worthless,

profitless prince; but payment came,

a prince with no results; but his payment came,

to the warrior honored, for all his woes. –

to the honored warrior, for all his woes. –

Then the bulwark-of-earls bade bring within,

Then the king commanded to be brought inside,

hardy chieftain, Hrethel's heirloom

the sturdy chief, Hrethel's heirloom

garnished with gold: no Geat e'er knew

decorated with gold: no Geat ever knew

in shape of a sword a statelier prize.

a better prize in the shape of a sword.

The brand he laid in Beowulf's lap;

The weapon he placed in Beowulf's lap'

and of hides assigned him seven thousand,

and granted him seven thousand plots of land,

with house and high-seat. They held in common

with buildings and a mansion. They shared

land alike by their line of birth,

much land by their common inheritance,

inheritance, home: but higher the king

their home: but the king was held higher

because of his rule o'er the realm itself.

because of his rule over the realm itself.

Now further it fell with the flight of years,

Now it happened, as the years went by,

with harryings horrid, that Hygelac perished,

and horrible conflict, that Hygelac died,

and Heardred, too, by hewing of swords
and Heardred, too, by the stabbing of swords

under the shield-wall slaughtered lay,
lay dead under the shield-wall,

when him at the van of his victor-folk
when he at the demand of his victorious people

sought hardy heroes, Heatho-Scilfings,
looking for hardy heroes, Heatho-Scilfings,

in arms o'erwhelming Hereric's nephew.
overwhelming Hereric's nephew with their weapons.

Then Beowulf came as king this broad
Then Beowulf became king this broad

realm to wield; and he ruled it well
realm to control; and he ruled it well

fifty winters, a wise old prince,
for fifty years, becoming a wise old prince,

warding his land, until One began
protecting his land, until One began

in the dark of night, a Dragon, to rage.

in the dark of night, a Dragon, to attack.

In the grave on the hill a hoard it guarded,

In the cave on the hill it guarded a hoard,

in the stone-barrow steep. A strait path reached it,

in the steep stone-barrow. A straight path reached it,

unknown to mortals. Some man, however,

unknown to other living things. Some man, however,

came by chance that cave within

came by chance to that cave, and inside it

to the heathen hoard. In hand he took

that evil hoard. In his hand he took

a golden goblet, nor gave he it back,

a golden goblet, and did not give it back,

stole with it away, while the watcher slept,

stole it away, while the watcher slept,

by thievish wiles: for the warden's wrath

by clever thieving: for the warden's wrath

prince and people must pay betimes!

the prince and people must later pay!

~*~

Section XXX

THAT way he went with no will of his own,

HE went that way without intending to,

in danger of life, to the dragon's hoard,

endangering his life, to the dragon's hoard,

but for pressure of peril, some prince's thane.

but escaping from danger, some prince's man.

He fled in fear the fatal scourge,

He fled in fear of death,

seeking shelter, a sinful man,

hoping to find shelter, a sinful man,

and entered in. At the awful sight

and went in. At the awful sight

tottered that guest, and terror seized him;

the guest staggered, and terror seized him;

yet the wretched fugitive rallied anon

yet the wretched fugitive recovered himself

from fright and fear ere he fled away,

from fright and fear before he fled away,

and took the cup from that treasure-hoard.

and took that one cup from that treasure-hoard.

Of such besides there was store enough,

There was more than enough of other similar things,

heirlooms old, the earth below,

old heirlooms, under the earth,

which some earl forgotten, in ancient years,

which some forgotten noble, in ancient years,

left the last of his lofty race,

left the last of his mighty race,

heedfully there had hidden away,

had carefully hidden away there,

dearest treasure. For death of yore

most valuable treasure. For death already

had hurried all hence; and he alone

and taken the rest; and he alone

left to live, the last of the clan,

was left to live, the last of the clan,

weeping his friends, yet wished to bide

crying over his friends, yet wished to continue

warding the treasure, his one delight,

guarding the treasure, his one delight,

though brief his respite. The barrow, new-ready,

though he did not have long left. The barrow, newly ready,

to strand and sea-waves stood anear,

stood near the strand and sea-waves,

hard by the headland, hidden and closed;

close to the headland, hidden and shut;

there laid within it his lordly heirlooms

and placed inside it his lordly heirlooms

and heaped hoard of heavy gold

and the piled plenty of heavy gold

that warden of rings. Few words he spake:

that guardian of jewels. He spoke a few words:

"Now hold thou, earth, since heroes may not,

"Now you hold it, earth, since heroes may not,

what earls have owned! Lo, erst from thee

what earls have owned! Listen, from you before

brave men brought it! But battle-death seized

brave men brought it! But death in battle caught

and cruel killing my clansmen all,

and cruelly killed all my clansmen,

robbed them of life and a liegeman's joys.

robbed them of life and a loyal man's joys.

None have I left to lift the sword,

I have none left to lift the sword,

or to cleanse the carven cup of price,

or clean the costly carved cup,

beaker bright. My brave are gone.

the bright beaker. My brave soldiers are gone.

And the helmet hard, all haughty with gold,

And the hard helmet, all proud with gold,

shall part from its plating. Polishers sleep

shall separate from its plating. The polishers are dead

who could brighten and burnish the battle-mask;

who could brighten and burnish that battle-helmet;

and those weeds of war that were wont to brave

and those war clothes that so often braved

over bicker of shields the bite of steel

over the clash of shields that stab of steel

rust with their bearer. The ringed mail

rust with their armor. The ringed chain-mail

fares not far with famous chieftain,

does not go far with the famous chief,

at side of hero! No harp's delight,

at the side of the hero! No delightful harp music,

no glee-wood's gladness! No good hawk now

no gladness of that instrument! No good falcon now

flies through the hall! Nor horses fleet

flies through the hall! No fast horses

stamp in the burgstead! Battle and death

stamp in the stable! Battle and death

the flower of my race have reft away."

has taken away the glory of my race."

Mournful of mood, thus he moaned his woe,

Mournfully, in this way he cried over his woe,

alone, for them all, and unblithe wept

alone, for them all, and unhappily cried

by day and by night, till death's fell wave

by day and by night, until death's terrible wave

o'erwhelmed his heart. His hoard-of-bliss

overwhelmed his heart. His beloved hoard

that old ill-doer open found,

that old ill-doer found open,

who, blazing at twilight the barrows haunteth,

who, haunting the barrows in the twilight,

naked foe-dragon flying by night

the naked evil dragon flying by night

folded in fire: the folk of earth

folded in fire: the people of the earth

dread him sore. 'Tis his doom to seek

deeply dreaded him. It was his doom to search out

hoard in the graves, and heathen gold

hoards in graves, and evil gold

to watch, many-wintered: nor wins he thereby!

to watch over the many years: though he made no profit from it!

Powerful this plague-of-the-people thus

The plague-of-the-people in this way powerfully

held the house of the hoard in earth
held the hoard in the ground

three hundred winters; till One aroused
for three hundred years; until One brought out

wrath in his breast, to the ruler bearing
anger in his heart, carrying to the ruler

that costly cup, and the king implored
that costly cup, and begged the king

for bond of peace. So the barrow was plundered,
for a promise of protection. So the barrow was plundered,

borne off was booty. His boon was granted
the treasure taken. His request was granted

that wretched man; and his ruler saw
that wretched man; and his ruler knew

first time what was fashioned in far-off days.
for the first time what came to be long ago.

When the dragon awoke, new woe was kindled.
When the dragon awoke, new sorrows began.

O'er the stone he snuffed. The stark-heart found

He sniffed the stone. The cold-hearted creature found

footprint of foe who so far had gone

the footprint of the foe who had taken it

in his hidden craft by the creature's head. –

in his hidden cleverness past the creature's head. –

So may the undoomed easily flee

So may those not doomed easily escape

evils and exile, if only he gain

evils and exile, if only they gain

the grace of The Wielder! -- That warden of gold

the grace of God! – That guardian of gold

o'er the ground went seeking, greedy to find

went over the ground, searching, greedy to find

the man who wrought him such wrong in sleep.

the man who did him such wrong as he slept.

Savage and burning, the barrow he circled

Savage and burning, he circled the barrow

all without; nor was any there,

all around; and no one was there,

none in the waste.... Yet war he desired,

none in the barren place…Yet he wanted war,

was eager for battle. The barrow he entered,

was eager for battle. He entered the barrow,

sought the cup, and discovered soon

looking for the cup, and soon discovered

that some one of mortals had searched his treasure,

that some human had taken a bit of his treasure,

his lordly gold. The guardian waited

his lordly gold. The guardian [of treasure] waited,

ill-enduring till evening came;

impatiently waiting until evening came;

boiling with wrath was the barrow's keeper,

the barrow's keeper was boiling with anger

and fain with flame the foe to pay

and intended to pay the foe with fire

for the dear cup's loss. -- Now day was fled

for the precious cup's loss. – Now the sun had set

as the worm had wished. By its wall no more

as the dragon desired. By its wall no more

was it glad to bide, but burning flew

did it wish to stay, but flew burning

folded in flame: a fearful beginning

folded in flame: a frightening thing

for sons of the soil; and soon it came,

for the farmers; and soon it came,

in the doom of their lord, to a dreadful end.

in the fate of their lord [Beowulf], to a dreadful end.

~*~

Section XXXI

THEN the baleful fiend its fire belched out,

THEN the awful fiend breathed out flames,

and bright homes burned. The blaze stood high

and the pretty homes burned. The blaze shot high

all landsfolk frighting. No living thing

frightening the people. No living thing

would that loathly one leave as aloft it flew.

would that loathsome one leave alive as it flew away.

Wide was the dragon's warring seen,

The dragon's aggression was widely witnessed,

its fiendish fury far and near,

its fiendish fury both far and near,

as the grim destroyer those Geatish people

as the grim destroyer attacked those Geats

hated and hounded. To hidden lair,

hating and harassing them. To its hidden lair,

to its hoard it hastened at hint of dawn.

to its hoard it hurried as the morning dawned.

Folk of the land it had lapped in flame,

People of that land had been enveloped in flames,

with bale and brand. In its barrow it trusted,

with evil and aggression. It trusted in its cave,

its battling and bulwarks: that boast was vain!

its fortifications: that belief turned out wrong!

To Beowulf then the bale was told

To Beowulf then the bad news was brought

quickly and truly: the king's own home,

quickly and truthfully: the kings's own home

of buildings the best, in brand-waves melted,

the best of buildings, was scorched by the dragon,

that gift-throne of Geats. To the good old man

that great throne of Geats. To the good old man

sad in heart, 'twas heaviest sorrow.

sad in heart, it was the heaviest sorrow.

The sage assumed that his sovran God

The wise man assumed that is sovereign God

he had angered, breaking ancient law,

he had angered by breaking ancient law,

and embittered the Lord. His breast within

and brining bitterness from the Lord. His heart within

with black thoughts welled, as his wont was never.

welled up with dark thoughts, which rarely happened to him.

The folk's own fastness that fiery dragon

The people's own fortress that fiery dragon

with flame had destroyed, and the stronghold all

had destroyed with flames, and the stronghold all

washed by waves; but the warlike king,

washed by waves; but the warrior king,

prince of the Weders, plotted vengeance.

prince of the Weders, planned revenge.

Warriors'-bulwark, he bade them work

Fortifications, he told them to make

all of iron -- the earl's commander –

all of iron – the commander of the nobles –

a war-shield wondrous: well he knew

a wonderful war-shield: he knew well

that forest-wood against fire were worthless,

that forest-wood was worthless against fire,

linden could aid not. -- Atheling brave,

timber could not help. – Brave warrior

he was fated to finish this fleeting life,

he was fated to finish this short and quickly-passing life,

his days on earth, and the dragon with him,

his days alive, and the dragon would die with him,

though long it had watched o'er the wealth of the hoard! –

though it had watched over the wealth of the hoard for a long time! –

Shame he reckoned it, sharer-of-rings,

He considered it shameful, the sharer-of-rings,

to follow the flyer-afar with a host,

to follow the dragon with an army,

a broad-flung band; nor the battle feared he,

a band of soliders; he did not fear the battle,

nor deemed he dreadful the dragon's warring,

or think the dragon's fighting dreadful,

its vigor and valor: ventures desperate

its vigor and valor: on desperate adventures

he had passed a-plenty, and perils of war,

he had survived plenty, and the dangers of war,

contest-crash, since, conqueror proud,

and conflict, since, the proud conquerer,

Hrothgar's hall he had wholly purged,

he had entirely rid Hrothgar's hall of vermin,

and in grapple had killed the kin of Grendel,

and in unarmed combat had killed the mother of Grendel,

loathsome breed! Not least was that

loathsome breed! And still dangerous was that

of hand-to-hand fights where Hygelac fell,

hand-to-hand fight where Hygelac was killed,

when the ruler of Geats in rush of battle,

when the ruler of Geats in the chaos of battle,

lord of his folk, in the Frisian land,

lord of his people, in the Frisian land,

son of Hrethel, by sword-draughts died,

son of Hrethel, died of sword-wounds,

by brands down-beaten. Thence Beowulf fled

beaten down by weapons. From there Beowulf escaped

through strength of himself and his swimming power,

through his own strength and his swimming power,

though alone, and his arms were laden with thirty

though alone, and his arms were full of thirty

coats of mail, when he came to the sea!

sets of chain-mail, when he reached the sea!

Nor yet might Hetwaras haughtily boast

And Hetwaras could not proudly brag

their craft of contest, who carried against him

their skill in fighting, who carried against him

shields to the fight: but few escaped

shields to the fight: but few of them escaped

from strife with the hero to seek their homes!

from conflict with the hero to return home!

Then swam over ocean Ecgtheow's son

Then Ecgtheow's son swam over the ocean

lonely and sorrowful, seeking his land,

alone and sorrowful, seeking his land,

where Hygd made him offer of hoard and realm,

where Hygd offered him the treasure and the kingdom,

rings and royal-seat, reckoning naught

the rings and the throne, not believing in

the strength of her son to save their kingdom

the strength of her son to save their kingdom

from hostile hordes, after Hygelac's death.

from huge hostile armies, after Hygelac's death.

No sooner for this could the stricken ones

No sooner for this could the bereaved ones

in any wise move that atheling's mind

in any way change that warrior's mind

over young Heardred's head as lord

to replace young Heardred as lord

and ruler of all the realm to be:

and ruler to be of all that realm:

yet the hero upheld him with helpful words,

yet the hero encouraged him with helpful words,

aided in honor, till, older grown,

helped him honorably, until, when he had grown older

he wielded the Weder-Geats. -- Wandering exiles

he [Heardred] ruled over the Weder-Geats. – Wandering exiles

sought him o'er seas, the sons of Ohtere,

searched for him over the seas, the sons of Ohtere,

who had spurned the sway of the Scylfings'-helm

who had rejected the rule of the Scylfins' leader

the bravest and best that broke the rings,

the best and bravest that distributed rings,

in Swedish land, of the sea-kings' line,

in Sweden, of the sea-kings' descent

haughty hero. Hence Heardred's end.

The proud hero. This was how Heardred died.

For shelter he gave them, sword-death came,

For he gave them shelter, and sword-death came,

the blade's fell blow, to bairn of Hygelac;

the blade's terrible blow, to the son of Hygelac;

but the son of Ongentheow sought again

but the son of Ongentheow searched again

house and home when Heardred fell,

for his own home when Heardred was killed,

leaving Beowulf lord of Geats

leaving Beowulf as the new lord of Geats

and gift-seat's master. -- A good king he!

and master of the throne. – He was a good king!

~*~

Section XXXII

THE fall of his lord he was fain to requite

THE death of his lord he planned to avenge

in after days; and to Eadgils he proved

in following times; and to Eadgils he showed himself

friend to the friendless, and forces sent

a friend to the friendless, and sent forces

over the sea to the son of Ohtere,

over the sea to Ohtere's son [Eadgils]

weapons and warriors: well repaid he

weapons and warriors: he well repaid

those care-paths cold when the king he slew.

those cold troubles when he killed the king.

Thus safe through struggles the son of Ecgtheow

In this way the son of Ecgtheow safely through struggles

had passed a plenty, through perils dire,

had survived plenty, through terrible dangers,

with daring deeds, till this day was come

with daring deeds, until this day had come

that doomed him now with the dragon to strive.

that fated him now to fight against the dragon.

With comrades eleven the lord of Geats

With eleven comrades the lord of Geats

swollen in rage went seeking the dragon.

filled with rage went searching for the dragon.

He had heard whence all the harm arose

He had heard from where all the harm came

and the killing of clansmen; that cup of price

and the killing of clansmen; that costly cup

on the lap of the lord had been laid by the finder.

on the lap of the lord had been placed by the finder.

In the throng was this one thirteenth man,

In the throng was this thirteenth man,

starter of all the strife and ill,

the starter of all this conflict and badness,

care-laden captive; cringing thence

the worried captive; cringing from there

forced and reluctant, he led them on

forced and reluctant, he let them there

till he came in ken of that cavern-hall,

till he came within knowledge of that cavern-hall

the barrow delved near billowy surges,

the barrow dug near the billowing waves,

flood of ocean. Within 'twas full

the flood of the ocean. Inside it was full

of wire-gold and jewels; a jealous warden,

of wire-gold and jewels; a careful guard,

warrior trusty, the treasures held,

a trusty warrior, held the treasures,

lurked in his lair. Not light the task

lurked in his lair. Not easy the task

of entrance for any of earth-born men!

of entering for any man!

Sat on the headland the hero king,

The hero king sat on the headland,

spake words of hail to his hearth-companions,

spoke warm words to his hearth-companions,

gold-friend of Geats. All gloomy his soul,

the gold-friend of the Geats. His soul was all gloomy,

wavering, death-bound. Wyrd full nigh

uncertain, headed for death. Fate completely

stood ready to greet the gray-haired man,

stood ready to greet the elderly man,

to seize his soul-hoard, sunder apart

to seize his soul, slice apart

life and body. Not long would be

life and body. For only a short time would

the warrior's spirit enwound with flesh.

the warrior's spirit remain in his flesh.

Beowulf spake, the bairn of Ecgtheow: --

Beowulf spoke, the son of Ecgtheow: --

"Through store of struggles I strove in youth,

"Through plenty of struggles I fought in youth,

mighty feuds; I mind them all.

mighty feuds; I remember them all.

I was seven years old when the sovran of rings,

I was seven years old when the sovereign of rings,

friend-of-his-folk, from my father took me,

friend-of-his-folk, took me from my father,

had me, and held me, Hrethel the king,

cared for me, and held me, Hrethel the king,

with food and fee, faithful in kinship.

with food and money, faithful in family.

Ne'er, while I lived there, he loathlier found me,

Never, while I lived there, he thought me less,

bairn in the burg, than his birthright sons,

a child in the city, than his natural sons,

Herebeald and Haethcyn and Hygelac mine.

Herebeald and Haethcyn and my Hygelac.

For the eldest of these, by unmeet chance,

For the eldest of these, by unlucky chance,

by kinsman's deed, was the death-bed strewn,

by kinsman's deed, was brought to his deathbed,

when Haethcyn killed him with horny bow,

when Haethcyn [accidentally] killed him with a bow,

his own dear liege laid low with an arrow,

his own dear brother laid low with an arrow,

missed the mark and his mate shot down,

missed the target and shot his friend,

one brother the other, with bloody shaft.

one brother the other, with a bloody arrow.

A feeless fight, and a fearful sin,

A useless fight, and a fearful sin,

horror to Hrethel; yet, hard as it was,

horrible to Hrethel; yet, hard as it was,

unavenged must the atheling die!

the warrior could not be avenged!

Too awful it is for an aged man

It is too awful for an old man

to bide and bear, that his bairn so young

to bear, that his child so young

rides on the gallows. A rime he makes,

goes to the gallows. A rhyme he makes,

sorrow-song for his son there hanging

a sorrowful song for his son there hanging

as rapture of ravens; no rescue now

as food for ravens; no rescue now

can come from the old, disabled man!

can come from the old, disabled man [his father]!

Still is he minded, as morning breaks,

Still he remembers, as morning breaks,

of the heir gone elsewhere; another he hopes not

of the heir gone away; another he hopes not

he will bide to see his burg within

that he will live to see within his city

as ward for his wealth, now the one has found

as a protector of his wealth, now the one has found

doom of death that the deed incurred.

doom of death brought about by the deed.

Forlorn he looks on the lodge of his son,

All sad he looks on the home of his son,

wine-hall waste and wind-swept chambers

the empty wine-hall and the wind-swept rooms

reft of revel. The rider sleepeth,

bereft of noise and fun. The ride sleeps in death,

the hero, far-hidden; no harp resounds,

the hero, hidden far away; no harp resounds,

in the courts no wassail, as once was heard.

in the courts no cheering, as once was heart.

~*~

Section XXXIII

"THEN he goes to his chamber, a grief-song chants

"THEN he goes to his room, chanting a grief-song

alone for his lost. Too large all seems,

alone for what he has lost. It seems too large,

homestead and house. So the helmet-of-Weders

his home and house. So the leader of Weders

hid in his heart for Herebeald

for the loss of Herebeald hid in his heart

waves of woe. No way could he take

waves of woe. There was no way he could take

to avenge on the slayer slaughter so foul;

to avenge such a terrible slaughter on the killer;

nor e'en could he harass that hero at all

he could not even harass the hero at all

with loathing deed, though he loved him not.

with hateful actions, though he no longer loved him.

And so for the sorrow his soul endured,

And so for all the sorrow his soul endured,

men's gladness he gave up and God's light chose.

he gave up men's gladness and chose God's light.

Lands and cities he left his sons

He left his sons lands and cities

(as the wealthy do) when he went from earth.

(as the wealthy do) when he left the earth.

There was strife and struggle 'twixt Swede and Geat

There was conflict and struggle between the Swedes and the Geats

o'er the width of waters; war arose,

over the sea; war arose,

hard battle-horror, when Hrethel died,

horrible battle, when Hrethel died,

and Ongentheow's offspring grew

and Ongentheow's children grew

strife-keen, bold, nor brooked o'er the seas

eager for war, bold, and did not follow over the seas

pact of peace, but pushed their hosts

peace treaties, but pushed their hosts

to harass in hatred by Hreosnabeorh.

to hatefully harass by Hreosnabeorh.

Men of my folk for that feud had vengeance,

My people had revenge for that feud,

for woful war ('tis widely known),

for woeful war (it is widely known),

though one of them bought it with blood of his heart,

though one of them bought it with his blood,

a bargain hard: for Haethcyn proved

a hard bargain: for Haethcyn it turned out

fatal that fray, for the first-of-Geats.

to be a fatal fight, for the first-of-Geats.

At morn, I heard, was the murderer killed

In the morning, I heard, the murderer was killed

by kinsman for kinsman, with clash of sword,

by kinsman for kinsman, in a sword-fight,

when Ongentheow met Eofor there.

when Ongentheow met Eofor at the battle.

Wide split the war-helm: wan he fell,

The war-helmet split wide: he fell weakly,

hoary Scylfing; the hand that smote him

the sturdy Scylfing; the hand that struck him

of feud was mindful, nor flinched from the death-blow.

remembering the feud, not flinching from the death-blow.

-- "For all that he gave me, my gleaming sword

-- "For all that he gave me, my shining sword

repaid him at war, -- such power I wielded, --

repaid him at war, -- such power I used, --

for lordly treasure: with land he entrusted me,

for lordly treasure: he had trusted me with land,

homestead and house. He had no need

homestead and a house. He had no need

from Swedish realm, or from Spear-Dane folk,

of anything from Sweden, or from the Spear-Dane folk,

or from men of the Gifths, to get him help, --

or from men of the Gifths, to give him help, --

some warrior worse for wage to buy!

some warriors for the wages one pays them!

Ever I fought in the front of all,

I fought constantly in the front of everyone,

sole to the fore; and so shall I fight

alone in the front; and in this way I will fight

while I bide in life and this blade shall last
while I am still alive and this sword shall last

that early and late hath loyal proved
that has been loyal to me

since for my doughtiness Daeghrefn fell,
since because of my endurance Daeghrefn died,

slain by my hand, the Hugas' champion.
killed by my hand, the Hugas' champion.

Nor fared he thence to the Frisian king
He did not go from there to the Frisian king

with the booty back, and breast-adornments;
taking treasures back;

but, slain in struggle, that standard-bearer
but, killed in the struggle, that flag bearer

fell, atheling brave. Not with blade was he slain,
fell, brave warrior. He was not killed with a blade,

but his bones were broken by brawny gripe,
but his bones were broken by my strong grip,

his heart-waves stilled. -- The sword-edge now,

his heartbeat stopped. – The sword-edge now,

hard blade and my hand, for the hoard shall strive."

the hard blade and my hand, shall try to get the hoard."

Beowulf spake, and a battle-vow made

Beowulf spoke, and made a battle-vow

his last of all: "I have lived through many

his last of all: "I have survived many

wars in my youth; now once again,

wars in my life, since I was young; now once again,

old folk-defender, feud will I seek,

an old defender of the people, I will pursue a feud

do doughty deeds, if the dark destroyer

do enduring deeds, if the dark destroyer

forth from his cavern come to fight me!"

comes out of his cavern to fight me!"

Then hailed he the helmeted heroes all,

Then he said goodbye to all the helmeted heroes,

for the last time greeting his liegemen dear,

speaking for the last time to his dear men,

comrades of war: "I should carry no weapon,

comrades of war: "I would carry no weapon,

no sword to the serpent, if sure I knew

no sword against the dragon, if I knew for sure

how, with such enemy, else my vows

how, with such an enemy, so that my promise

I could gain as I did in Grendel's day.

I could keep as I did when I fought Grendel.

But fire in this fight I must fear me now,

But I must fear fire in this fight now,

and poisonous breath; so I bring with me

and poisonous breath; so I will bring with me

breastplate and board. From the barrow's keeper

my breastplate and shield. From the barrow's keeper

no footbreadth flee I. One fight shall end

I will not run even one step. One fight shall end

our war by the wall, as Wyrd allots,

our war by the wall, as Fate decides,

all mankind's master. My mood is bold

all humanity's master. My mood is bold

but forbears to boast o'er this battling-flyer.

but will refrain from boasting about this battle.

-- Now abide by the barrow, ye breastplate-mailed,

-- Now wait by the barrow, you who are armored in breastplates,

ye heroes in harness, which of us twain

you heroes in gear, which one of us

better from battle-rush bear his wounds.

better survives his wounds from the battle.

Wait ye the finish. The fight is not yours,

You wait until it is over. The fight is not yours,

nor meet for any but me alone

and not suitable for anyone but me alone

to measure might with this monster here

to measure my strength with this monster here

and play the hero. Hardily I

and act as the hero. Hardily I

shall win that wealth, or war shall seize,

shall win that wealth, or war shall take me,

cruel killing, your king and lord!"

cruelly killing your king and lord!"

Up stood then with shield the sturdy champion

The sturdy champion stood then with his shield

stayed by the strength of his single manhood,

encouraged by the strength of his manhood,

and hardy 'neath helmet his harness bore

and hardy beneath the helmet carried his harness

under cleft of the cliffs: no coward's path!

under the crack in the cliffs: no coward's path!

Soon spied by the wall that warrior chief,

The warrior chief soon spotted by the wall,

survivor of many a victory-field

survivor of many victorious battles

where foemen fought with furious clashings,

where enemies fought with tremendous noise,

an arch of stone; and within, a stream

an arch of stone; and inside, a stream

that broke from the barrow. The brooklet's wave

that flowed from the barrow. The brook's wave

was hot with fire. The hoard that way

was hot with fire. From that way to the hoard

he never could hope unharmed to near,

he could never hope to come near unharmed,

or endure those deeps, for the dragon's flame.

or endure those deeps, because of the dragon's flame.

Then let from his breast, for he burst with rage,

Then out of his chest, for he burst with rage,

the Weder-Geat prince a word outgo;

the Weder-Geat prince screamed;

stormed the stark-heart; stern went ringing

stormed the empty-hearted monster; it went ringing

and clear his cry 'neath the cliff-rocks gray.

and clear, his cry beneath the gray cliff-rocks.

The hoard-guard heard a human voice;

The guard of the hoard heard a human voice;

his rage was enkindled. No respite now

his rage awakened. No rest now

for pact of peace! The poison-breath

for any peace! The poisoned breath

of that foul worm first came forth from the cave,

of that dreadful dragon first came out of the cave,

hot reek-of-fight: the rocks resounded.

hot stench of the fight: the rocks resounded.

Stout by the stone-way his shield he raised,

Sturdy by the stone-way he raised his shield,

lord of the Geats, against the loathed-one;

lord of the Geats, against the hated one;

while with courage keen that coiled foe

while with eager courage that coiled foe

came seeking strife. The sturdy king

came looking for a fight. The sturdy king

had drawn his sword, not dull of edge,

had drawn his sharp sword,

heirloom old; and each of the two

an old heirloom; and both of them

felt fear of his foe, though fierce their mood.

felt fear of his foe, though their mood was fierce.

Stoutly stood with his shield high-raised

Sturdily stood, raising his shield high,

the warrior king, as the worm now coiled

the warrior king, as the dragon now coiled

together amain: the mailed-one waited.

together again: the armored one waited.

Now, spire by spire, fast sped and glided

Now, column by column, fast hurried and glided

that blazing serpent. The shield protected,

that blazing dragon. The shield protected,

soul and body a shorter while

his soul and body for a shorter time

for the hero-king than his heart desired

than the hero-king could have wanted

could his will have wielded the welcome respite

could his will have used the welcome rest

but once in his life! But Wyrd denied it,

only once in his life! But Fate denied it,

and victory's honors. -- His arm he lifted

and victory's honors. — He lifted his harm

lord of the Geats, the grim foe smote

lord of the Geats, and struck the grim foe

with atheling's heirloom. Its edge was turned

with the warrior's heirloom. Its edge bent

brown blade, on the bone, and bit more feebly

the brown blade, by the bone, and a bit more feebly

than its noble master had need of then

than its noble master needed it to at the moment

in his baleful stress. -- Then the barrow's keeper

in his awful stress. — Then the barrow's keeper

waxed full wild for that weighty blow,

grew fully wild for that weighty blow,

cast deadly flames; wide drove and far

threw deadly flames; drove wide and far

those vicious fires. No victor's glory

those vicious fires. No winner's glory

the Geats' lord boasted; his brand had failed,

the Geats' lord bragged; his weapon had failed,

naked in battle, as never it should,

naked in battle, as it never should have,

excellent iron! -- 'Twas no easy path

that excelled iron! – It was no easy path

that Ecgtheow's honored heir must tread

that Ecgthow's honored hear had to tread

over the plain to the place of the foe;

over the plain to the place of the enemy;

for against his will he must win a home

for against his will he must make a home

elsewhere far, as must all men, leaving

somewhere else far away, as all men must, leaving

this lapsing life! -- Not long it was

this temporary life! – It was not long

ere those champions grimly closed again.

before champions grimly closed again.

The hoard-guard was heartened; high heaved his breast

The guard of the hoard was encouraged; puffed up his chest

once more; and by peril was pressed again,

once more; and was in danger again,

enfolded in flames, the folk-commander!

surrounded by flames, the commander of the people!

Nor yet about him his band of comrades,

And none yet of his band of comrades around him

sons of athelings, armed stood

the sons of warriors, stood with weapons

with warlike front: to the woods they bent them,

with a warlike attitude: they headed to the woods,

their lives to save. But the soul of one

to save their lives. But the soul of one

with care was cumbered. Kinship true

was worried. True kinship

can never be marred in a noble mind!

can never be damaged in a noble mind!

~*~

Section XXXIV

WIGLAF his name was, Weohstan's son,

HIS NAME was Wiglaf, Weohstan's son,

linden-thane loved, the lord of Scylfings,

loved by the thane, the lord of Scylfings,

Aelfhere's kinsman. His king he now saw

Aelfhere's kinsman. He now saw his king

with heat under helmet hard oppressed.

being in serious trouble from the heat under his helmet

He minded the prizes his prince had given him,

He remembered the prizes his prince had given him,

wealthy seat of the Waegmunding line,

the wealthy home of the Waegmunding family,

and folk-rights that his father owned.

and the rights that his father owned.

Not long he lingered. The linden yellow,

He did not linger long. The yellow linden,

his shield, he seized; the old sword he drew: --

his shield, he grabbed; he drew the old sword: --

as heirloom of Eanmund earth-dwellers knew it,

those on earth knew it as heirloom of Eanmund,

who was slain by the sword-edge, son of Ohtere,

who was killed by the sword, son of Ohtere,

friendless exile, erst in fray

the friendless exile, later in battle

killed by Weohstan, who won for his kin

killed by Weohstan, who won for his family

brown-bright helmet, breastplate ringed,

the bright brown helmet, a ringed breastplate,

old sword of Eotens, Onela's gift,

the old sword of Eotens, Onela's gift,

weeds of war of the warrior-thane,

war-clothes of the warrior,

battle-gear brave: though a brother's child

brave battle-gear: though a nephew

had been felled, the feud was unfelt by Onela.

had been killed, Onela did not pursue the feud.

For winters this war-gear Weohstan kept,

Woehstan kept this war-gear for years,

breastplate and board, till his bairn had grown

the breastplate and shield, until his child had grown

earlship to earn as the old sire did:

to earn high rank as his father did:

then he gave him, mid Geats, the gear of battle,

then he gave him the battle gear,

portion huge, when he passed from life,

a huge portion, when he passed from life,

fared aged forth. For the first time now

died of old age. For the first time now

with his leader-lord the liegeman young

with his lord and leader the young liegeman

was bidden to share the shock of battle.

was called upon to share in battle.

Neither softened his soul, nor the sire's bequest

His soul was not soft, and his father's bequest

weakened in war. So the worm found out

not weakened in war. That's what the dragon found out

when once in fight the foes had met!

when he met both his enemies in the fight!

Wiglaf spake, -- and his words were sage;

Wigllaf spoke, and his words were wise;

sad in spirit, he said to his comrades: --

regretfully, he said to his comrades: --

"I remember the time, when mead we took,

"I remember the time, when we drank mead

what promise we made to this prince of ours

what promises we made to our prince

in the banquet-hall, to our breaker-of-rings,

in the banquet-hall, to our giver of wealth,

for gear of combat to give him requital,

in exchange for combat gear to repay him

for hard-sword and helmet, if hap should bring

for hard-sword and helmet, if chance should bring

stress of this sort! Himself who chose us

danger of this kind! He who chose us

from all his army to aid him now,

from all his army to help us now,

urged us to glory, and gave these treasures,

encouraged us to glory, and gave us each treasures,

because he counted us keen with the spear
because he thought us skilled with the spear

and hardy 'neath helm, though this hero-work
and hardy beneath the helmet, though these heroics

our leader hoped unhelped and alone
our leader hoped alone and without help

to finish for us, -- folk-defender
to finish for us, -- defender of the people

who hath got him glory greater than all men
who has got himself glory greater than all men

for daring deeds! Now the day is come
for daring deeds! Now today is the day

that our noble master has need of the might
that our noble master has need of the power

of warriors stout. Let us stride along
of strong warriors. Let us go

the hero to help while the heat is about him
to the hero to help while the heat is around him

glowing and grim! For God is my witness

glowing and grim! As God is my witness

I am far more fain the fire should seize

I would much rather the fire seized

along with my lord these limbs of mine!

my limbs along with my lord!

Unsuiting it seems our shields to bear

It seems unsuitable for us to carry our shields

homeward hence, save here we essay

homeward from here, unless we stay

to fell the foe and defend the life

destroy the dragon and defend the life

of the Weders' lord. I wot 'twere shame

of the Weders' lord. I think it would bring shame

on the law of our land if alone the king

to the law of the land if the king all alone

out of Geatish warriors woe endured

out of the Geatish warriors endured trouble

and sank in the struggle! My sword and helmet,

and died in the attempt! My sword and helmet,

breastplate and board, for us both shall serve!"

breastplate and shield, shall serve for us both!"

Through slaughter-reek strode he to succor his chieftain,

Through the stench of slaughter he strode to save his chief,

his battle-helm bore, and brief words spake: --

carrying his battle-helmet, and spoke briefly: --

"Beowulf dearest, do all bravely,

"Dearest Beowulf, do everything bravely,

as in youthful days of yore thou vowedst

as in youthful days long ago you vowed

that while life should last thou wouldst let no wise

that while life should last you would not let

thy glory droop! Now, great in deeds,

your glory weaken! Now, great in deeds,

atheling steadfast, with all thy strength

steadfast warrior, with all your strength

shield thy life! I will stand to help thee."

protect your life! I will stand to help you."

At the words the worm came once again,

At the words the dragon came once again,

murderous monster mad with rage,

the murderous monster crazed with rage,

with fire-billows flaming, its foes to seek,

its waves of fire flaming, to find its foes

the hated men. In heat-waves burned

the hated men. The head-waves burned

that board to the boss, and the breastplate failed

that shield to a stub, and the breastplate failed

to shelter at all the spear-thane young.

to shelter the young warrior at all.

Yet quickly under his kinsman's shield

Yet he quickly under his kinsman's shield

went eager the earl, since his own was now

went eagerly, since his own was now

all burned by the blaze. The bold king again

all burned by the blaze. The bold king once again

had mind of his glory: with might his glaive

was thinking of his glory: with great strength his sword

was driven into the dragon's head, --

was stabbed into the dragon's head, --

blow nerved by hate. But Naegling was shivered,

his blow driven by hate. But Naegling was snapped,

broken in battle was Beowulf's sword,

Beowulf's sword was broken in battle,

old and gray. 'Twas granted him not

old and gray. It was not granted him

that ever the edge of iron at all

that an iron weapon could ever at all

could help him at strife: too strong was his hand,

could help him in conflict: he was too strong,

so the tale is told, and he tried too far

so they say, and he pushed too hard

with strength of stroke all swords he wielded,

with the strength of his stroke all the swords he wielded,

though sturdy their steel: they steaded him nought.

though their steel was sturdy: they did not help him.

Then for the third time thought on its feud

Then for the third time thinking of its feud

that folk-destroyer, fire-dread dragon,

that man-killer, fire-dread dragon,

and rushed on the hero, where room allowed,

and rushed on the hero, when there was room,

battle-grim, burning; its bitter teeth

battle-grim, burning; its terrible teeth

closed on his neck, and covered him

closed on his neck, and covered him

with waves of blood from his breast that welled.

with waves of blood that welled from his chest.

~*~

Section XXXV

'TWAS now, men say, in his sovran's need

It was now, men say, in his sovereign's need

that the earl made known his noble strain,

that the earl showed his inner nobility,

craft and keenness and courage enduring.

his intelligence and eagerness and enduring courage.

Heedless of harm, though his hand was burned,

Ignoring the danger, though his hand was burned,

hardy-hearted, he helped his kinsman.

strong hearted, he helped his kinsman.

A little lower the loathsome beast

A little lower the terrible beast

he smote with sword; his steel drove in

he struck with his sword; his steel sank in

bright and burnished; that blaze began

bright and polished; that blaze began

to lose and lessen. At last the king

to lighten and lessen. At last the king

wielded his wits again, war-knife drew,

came to his senses, pulling out a knife,

a biting blade by his breastplate hanging,

a sharp blade hanging by his breastplaste,

and the Weders'-helm smote that worm asunder,

and the king of Weders cut that dragon in two,

felled the foe, flung forth its life.

felled the foe, threw away its life.

So had they killed it, kinsmen both,

So they had killed it, both kinsmen,

athelings twain: thus an earl should be

two warriors: this is how a nobleman should be

in danger's day! -- Of deeds of valor

in times of danger! – Of valiant deeds

this conqueror's-hour of the king was last,

this was the king's last conquest,

of his work in the world. The wound began,

his final accomplishment. The wound began;

which that dragon-of-earth had erst inflicted,

which that earth-dragon had earlier inflicted,

to swell and smart; and soon he found

to swell and sting; and soon he found

in his breast was boiling, baleful and deep,

that in his chest was boiling, bad and deep,

pain of poison. The prince walked on,

the pain of poison. The prince walked on,

wise in his thought, to the wall of rock;

thinking wisely, to the wall of rock;

then sat, and stared at the structure of giants,

then sat, and stared at the construction of giants,

where arch of stone and steadfast column

where arches of stone and sturdy columns

upheld forever that hall in earth.

held up forever that hall underground.

Yet here must the hand of the henchman peerless

Yet here the hand of the matchless henchmen must

lave with water his winsome lord,

wash with water his loveable lord,

the king and conqueror covered with blood,

the blood-covered king and conqueror,

with struggle spent, and unspan his helmet.

exhausted with struggle, and unclasp his helmet.

Beowulf spake in spite of his hurt,

Beowulf spoke despite his injuries,

his mortal wound; full well he knew

his mortal wound; he knew full well

his portion now was past and gone

his time now was past and gone

of earthly bliss, and all had fled

of earthly bliss, and it was ended

of his file of days, and death was near:

of his number of days, and death was near:

"I would fain bestow on son of mine

"I would give to a son of mine

this gear of war, were given me now

this war gear, if it had been given to me now

that any heir should after me come

that any heir should come after me

of my proper blood. This people I ruled

of my descent. This people I ruled

fifty winters. No folk-king was there,

for fifty years. There was no king,

none at all, of the neighboring clans

none at all, of the nearby clans

who war would wage me with 'warriors'-friends'

who would try to start a war against me

and threat me with horrors. At home I bided

and threaten me with horrors. At home I accepted

what fate might come, and I cared for mine own;

what fate might come, and I cared for my people;

feuds I sought not, nor falsely swore

I did not look for fights, or ever lied

ever on oath. For all these things,

and gave false oath. For all these things,

though fatally wounded, fain am I!

though fatally wounded, I am glad!

From the Ruler-of-Man no wrath shall seize me,

From God no anger will trouble me

when life from my frame must flee away,

when life must escape my body,

for killing of kinsmen! Now quickly go

for killing kinsmen! Now quickly go

and gaze on that hoard 'neath the hoary rock,

and gaze on that hoard beneath the sturdy rock,

Wiglaf loved, now the worm lies low,

beloved Wiglaf, now the dragon is dead,

sleeps, heart-sore, of his spoil bereaved.

sleeps, heart-sore, robbed of his treasure.

And fare in haste. I would fain behold

And go quickly. I want to look

the gorgeous heirlooms, golden store,

at the gorgeous heirlooms, the stored gold,

have joy in the jewels and gems, lay down

take joy in the jewels and gems, lay down

softlier for sight of this splendid hoard

more softly because of the sight of this splendid hoard

my life and the lordship I long have held.

my life, and the lordship I have held so long.

Section XXXVI

I HAVE heard that swiftly the son of Weohstan

I HAVE heard that the son of Weohstan quickly

at wish and word of his wounded king, --

at the wish and command of his wounded king, --

war-sick warrior, -- woven mail-coat,

the war-sick warrior, -- woven chain-mail

battle-sark, bore 'neath the barrow's roof.

battle-cloth, took beneath the barrow's roof.

Then the clansman keen, of conquest proud,

Then the eager clansman, proud of conquest,

passing the seat, saw store of jewels

passing the opening, saw the pile of jewels

and glistening gold the ground along;

and glistening gold along the ground;

by the wall were marvels, and many a vessel

by the wall were marvles, and many a cup

in the den of the dragon, the dawn-flier old:

in the den of the dragon, the old dawn-flier:

unburnished bowls of bygone men

unpolished bowls of men from long ago

reft of richness; rusty helms
having lost their richness; rusty helmets

of the olden age; and arm-rings many
of the olden days; and many arm-rings

wondrously woven. -- Such wealth of gold,
wonderfully woven. – Such a wealth of gold,

booty from barrow, can burden with pride
prize from the barrow, can fill with pride

each human wight: let him hide it who will! –
each human being: let him hide it who wishes! –

His glance too fell on a gold-wove banner
His glance also fell on a golden woven banner

high o'er the hoard, of handiwork noblest,
high over the hoard, of the noblest handiwork,

brilliantly broidered; so bright its gleam,
brilliantly embroidered; so bright its gleam,

all the earth-floor he easily saw
he easily saw all the earth-floor

and viewed all these vessels. No vestige now

and viewed all these vessels. No remnant now

was seen of the serpent: the sword had ta'en him.

remained of the dragon: the sword had taken him.

Then, I heard, the hill of its hoard was reft,

Then, I heard, the hill was robbed of its hoard,

old work of giants, by one alone;

old work of giants, by a lone man;

he burdened his bosom with beakers and plate

he burdened himself with beakers and plates

at his own good will, and the ensign took,

at his own good will, and took the flag,

brightest of beacons. -- The blade of his lord

brightest of beacons. – His lord's knife

-- its edge was iron -- had injured deep

-- its edge was iron – had deeply injured

one that guarded the golden hoard

the one that guarded the golden hoard

many a year and its murder-fire

for many years and its murderous fires

spread hot round the barrow in horror-billows

spread hot around the barrow in horrible waves

at midnight hour, till it met its doom.

in the night, until it met its doom.

Hasted the herald, the hoard so spurred him

The herald hurried, the hoard so encouraged him

his track to retrace; he was troubled by doubt,

to retrace his steps; he was troubled by doubt,

high-souled hero, if haply he'd find

the good hero, if by chance he'd find

alive, where he left him, the lord of Weders,

alive, where he left him, the king of the Weders,

weakening fast by the wall of the cave.

weakening and dying by the wall of the cave.

So he carried the load. His lord and king

So he carried off the load. His lord and king

he found all bleeding, famous chief

he found bleeding copiously, famous chief

at the lapse of life. The liegeman again

at the end of his life. The liegeman again

plashed him with water, till point of word

washed him with water, until a word

broke through the breast-hoard. Beowulf spake,

broke from his chest. Beowulf spoke,

sage and sad, as he stared at the gold. –

wise and sad, as he stared at the gold. –

"For the gold and treasure, to God my thanks,

"For the gold and treasure, I thank God,

to the Wielder-of-Wonders, with words I say,

the Almighty, with words I say,

for what I behold, to Heaven's Lord,

for what I see, to Heaven's Lord,

for the grace that I give such gifts to my folk

for the blessing that I am able to give such gifts to my people

or ever the day of my death be run!

for the way I died!

Now I've bartered here for booty of treasure

Now I have traded here for treasure

the last of my life, so look ye well

the last of my life, so take good care

to the needs of my land! No longer I tarry.

of the needs of my land! I will stay no longer.

A barrow bid ye the battle-fanned raise

Tell them to raise a barrow

for my ashes. 'Twill shine by the shore of the flood,

for my ashes. It will shine by the shore of the ocean,

to folk of mine memorial fair

a beautiful memorial to my people

on Hrones Headland high uplifted,

lifted up high on Hrones Headland

that ocean-wanderers oft may hail

that ocean travelers may often greet

Beowulf's Barrow, as back from far

Beowulf's Barrow, as back from far away

they drive their keels o'er the darkling wave."

they steer their ships over the dark waves."

From his neck he unclasped the collar of gold,

From his neck he unclasped the gold necklace,

valorous king, to his vassal gave it

the brave king, gave it to his man

with bright-gold helmet, breastplate, and ring,

with the bright gold helmet, breastplate, and ring,

to the youthful thane: bade him use them in joy.

to the youthful thane: told him to use them joyfully.

"Thou art end and remnant of all our race

"You are the end and the last remaining of all our race

the Waegmunding name. For Wyrd hath swept them,

the Waegmunding name. For Fate has taken them,

all my line, to the land of doom,

all my family line, to the land of doom,

earls in their glory: I after them go."

nobles in their glory: I am following after them."

This word was the last which the wise old man

These words were the last which the wise old man

harbored in heart ere hot death-waves

had in his heart before the hot death-waves

of balefire he chose. From his bosom fled

of the fire he had willingly gone to. From his chest escaped his soul to seek the saints' reward.

his soul to go to Heaven.

~*~

Section XXXVII

IT was heavy hap for that hero young

IT was a heavy burden for that young hero

on his lord beloved to look and find him

to look at his beloved lord and find him

lying on earth with life at end,

lying dead on the ground,

sorrowful sight. But the slayer too,

a sorrowful sight. But his killer, too,

awful earth-dragon, empty of breath,

the awful earth-dragon, also dead,

lay felled in fight, nor, fain of its treasure,

lay felled in the fight, and, despite all its treasure,

could the writhing monster rule it more.

the writhing monster could rule it no more.

For edges of iron had ended its days,

For the iron blades had ended its days

hard and battle-sharp, hammers' leaving;

hard and battle-sharp, made with hammers;

and that flier-afar had fallen to ground

and that far flier had fallen to the ground

hushed by its hurt, its hoard all near,
silenced by its injuries, its hoard all new,

no longer lusty aloft to whirl
no longer eager aloft to whirl

at midnight, making its merriment seen,
at night, making its merriment seen,

proud of its prizes: prone it sank
proud of its prizes: it sank limply

by the handiwork of the hero-king.
by the actions of the hero-king.

Forsooth among folk but few achieve,
Indeed, among people only a few achieve

-- though sturdy and strong, as stories tell me,
-- though they are sturdy and strong, as stories tell me,

and never so daring in deed of valor, --
and never so daring in valiant deeds, --

the perilous breath of a poison-foe
the dangerous breath of a poisonous foe

to brave, and to rush on the ring-board hall,

to brave, and to attack the ring-board hall,

whenever his watch the warden keeps

whenever the guardian is on watch

bold in the barrow. Beowulf paid

bold in his barrow. Beowulf paid

the price of death for that precious hoard;

with his life for that precious hoard;

and each of the foes had found the end

and each of the enemies had found the end

of this fleeting life.

of this temporary life.

Befell erelong

It happened before long

that the laggards in war the wood had left,

that those that avoided the fight had left the wood,

trothbreakers, cowards, ten together,

breakers of their promise, cowards, ten together,

fearing before to flourish a spear

fearing before to fight with a spear

in the sore distress of their sovran lord.

in the great distress of their sovereign lord.

Now in their shame their shields they carried,

Now, ashamed, they carried their shields,

armor of fight, where the old man lay;

their battle armor, where the old man lay;

and they gazed on Wiglaf. Wearied he sat

and they gazed on Wiglaf. Tired, he sat

at his sovran's shoulder, shieldsman good,

by his sovereign, the good shieldsman,

to wake him with water. Nowise it availed.

to wake him with water. It failed.

Though well he wished it, in world no more

However much he wished it, no longer in the world

could he barrier life for that leader-of-battles

could he help save the life of that leader-of-battles

nor baffle the will of all-wielding God.

or fight against the will of Almighty God.

Doom of the Lord was law o'er the deeds

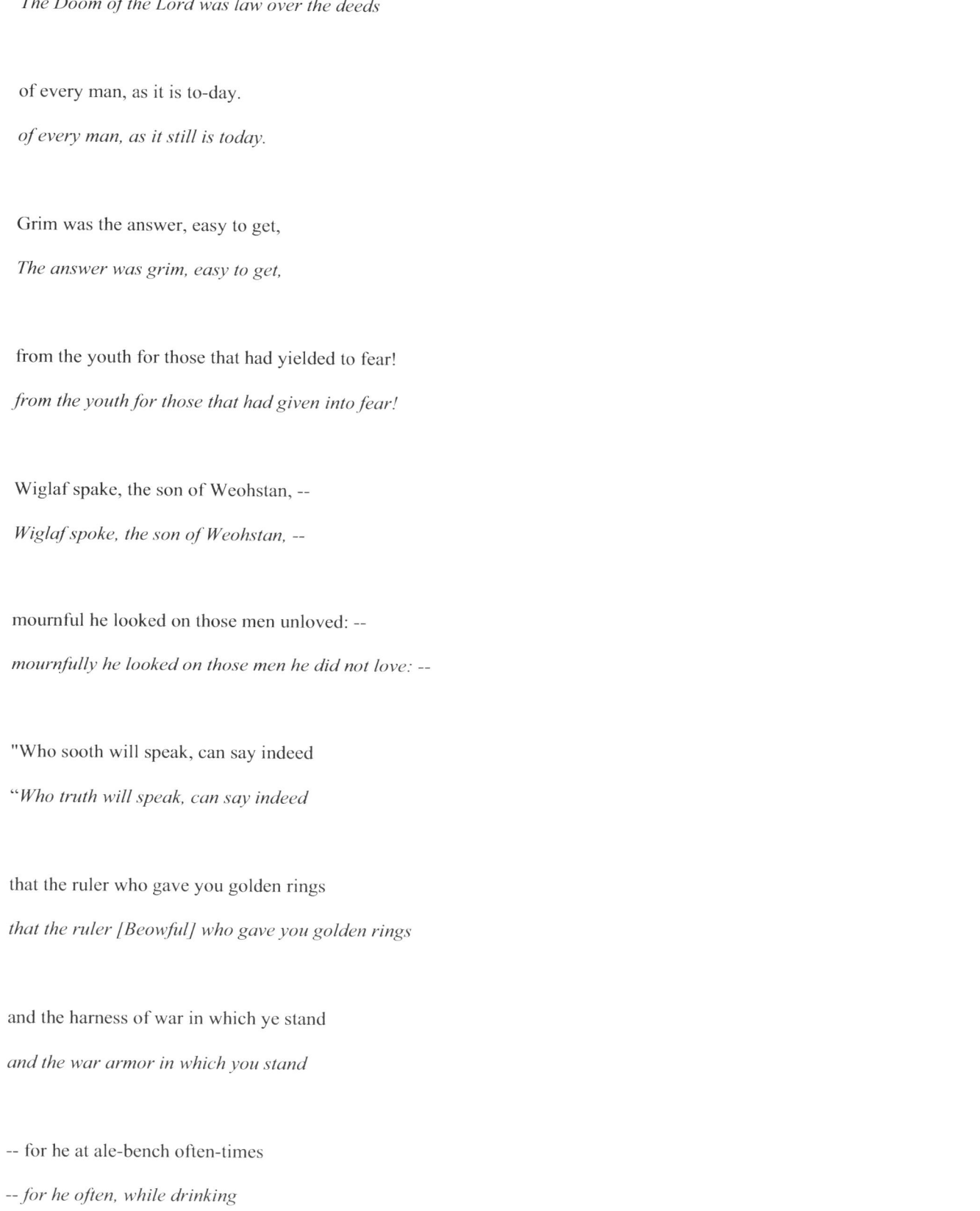

The Doom of the Lord was law over the deeds

of every man, as it is to-day.

of every man, as it still is today.

Grim was the answer, easy to get,

The answer was grim, easy to get,

from the youth for those that had yielded to fear!

from the youth for those that had given into fear!

Wiglaf spake, the son of Weohstan, --

Wiglaf spoke, the son of Weohstan, --

mournful he looked on those men unloved: --

mournfully he looked on those men he did not love: --

"Who sooth will speak, can say indeed

"Who truth will speak, can say indeed

that the ruler who gave you golden rings

that the ruler [Beowful] who gave you golden rings

and the harness of war in which ye stand

and the war armor in which you stand

-- for he at ale-bench often-times

-- for he often, while drinking

bestowed on hall-folk helm and breastplate,

gave to those in his hall helmets and breastplates,

lord to liegemen, the likeliest gear

lord to liegemen, the best-quality gear

which near of far he could find to give, --

which near or far he could find to give, --

threw away and wasted these weeds of battle,

threw away and wasted those tools of battle

on men who failed when the foemen came!

on men who failed when the enemy came!

Not at all could the king of his comrades-in-arms

Not at all could the king of his fellow fighters

venture to vaunt, though the Victory-Wielder,

try to claim, though the Victory-Wielder,

God, gave him grace that he got revenge

God, gave him a chance to get revenge

sole with his sword in stress and need.

all by himself with his sword in stress and need.

To rescue his life, 'twas little that I

To rescue his life, there was little that I

could serve him in struggle; yet shift I made

could help him in the struggle; yet I made do

(hopeless it seemed) to help my kinsman.

(it seemed hopeless) to help my kinsman.

Its strength ever waned, when with weapon I struck

Its strength weakened, when with my weapon I struck

that fatal foe, and the fire less strongly

that deadly foe, and the fire less strongly

flowed from its head. -- Too few the heroes

blazed from its mouth. – Too few the heroes

in throe of contest that thronged to our king!

during the conflict that rushed to surround our king!

Now gift of treasure and girding of sword,

Now the gifts of treasure and sword,

joy of the house and home-delight

the joy of your family and honor of home

shall fail your folk; his freehold-land

shall fail your people; his land

every clansman within your kin

every family member of yours

shall lose and leave, when lords high-born

shall lose and leave, when high-born lords

hear afar of that flight of yours,

hear from far away of that cowardly escape of yours,

a fameless deed. Yea, death is better

a dishonorable deed. Yes, death is better

for liegemen all than a life of shame!"

for all liegemen than a life of shame!"

~*~

Section XXXVIII

THAT battle-toil bade he at burg to announce,

AT the city they told him to announce the battle results,

at the fort on the cliff, where, full of sorrow,

at the fort of the cliff, where, full of sadness,

all the morning earls had sat,

nobles had sat all morning,

daring shieldsmen, in doubt of twain:

daring soldiers, with the double doubt:

would they wail as dead, or welcome home,

would they mourn as dead, or welcome home,

their lord beloved? Little kept back

their beloved lord? Nothing was left out

of the tidings new, but told them all,

of the news, but told them all,

the herald that up the headland rode. –

the herald that rode up the headland. –

"Now the willing-giver to Weder folk

"Now the willing giver to the Weder people

in death-bed lies; the Lord of Geats

lies dead; the Lord of Geats

on the slaughter-bed sleeps by the serpent's deed!

lies on this deathbed by the work of the dragon!

And beside him is stretched that slayer-of-men

And beside him is stretched that man-killer

with knife-wounds sick: no sword availed

full of knife-wounds: no sword worked

on the awesome thing in any wise

on the awful thing in any way

to work a wound. There Wiglaf sitteth,

to work a wound. Wiglaf sits there,

Weohstan's bairn, by Beowulf's side,

Weohstan's child, by Beowulf's side,

the living earl by the other dead,

the living noble by the dead one,

and heavy of heart a head-watch keeps

and heavy-hearted keeps a lookout

o'er friend and foe. -- Now our folk may look

over friend and foe. – Now our people must expect

for waging of war when once unhidden

war when it becomes widely known

to Frisian and Frank the fall of the king

to the Frisian and Franks that the king

is spread afar. -- The strife began

has died. – The conflict began

when hot on the Hugas Hygelac fell

when Hygelac passionately attacked the Hugas

and fared with his fleet to the Frisian land.

and went with his fleet of ships to the Frisian land.

Him there the Hetwaras humbled in war,

He there was defeated in war by the Hetwaras,

plied with such prowess their power o'erwhelming

fought against with such skill with their power overwhelming

that the bold-in-battle bowed beneath it

that the bold-in-battle was defeated by it

and fell in fight. To his friends no wise

and fell in fight. To his friends in no way

could that earl give treasure! And ever since

could that noble give treasure! And ever since

the Merowings' favor has failed us wholly.

the alliance with the Merowings' has completely failed us.

Nor aught expect I of peace and faith

I expect no peace or trust

from Swedish folk. 'Twas spread afar

from the Swedes. It was spread afar

how Ongentheow reft at Ravenswood

how Ogentheow took at Ravenswood

Haethcyn Hrethling of hope and life,

Haethcyn Hrethling's hope and life,

when the folk of Geats for the first time sought

when the folk of Geats for the first time tried to get

in wanton pride the Warlike-Scylfings.

in uncalled-for pride the Warlike-Scylfings.

Soon the sage old sire of Ohtere,

Soon the wise old father of Ohtere,

ancient and awful, gave answering blow;

old and terrible, struck back;

the sea-king he slew, and his spouse redeemed,

he killed the sea-king, and redeemed his spouse,

his good wife rescued, though robbed of her gold,

rescued his good wife, though she was robbed of her gold,

mother of Ohtere and Onela.

the mother of Ohtere and Onela.

Then he followed his foes, who fled before him

Then he followed his foes, who ran away from him

sore beset and stole their way,

terribly troubled and sneaked away,

bereft of a ruler, to Ravenswood.

having lost their ruler, to Ravenswood.

With his host he besieged there what swords had left,

With his army he besieged there what soldiers remained,

the weary and wounded; woes he threatened

the weary and wounded; he threatened woes

the whole night through to that hard-pressed throng:

all night to that hard-pressed crowd,

some with the morrow his sword should kill,

some his sword would kill in the morning,

some should go to the gallows-tree

some would go to the gallows

for rapture of ravens. But rescue came

to become food for ravens. But rescue came

with dawn of day for those desperate men

at sunrise for that desperate men

when they heard the horn of Hygelac sound,

when the heard the horn of Hygelac blow,

tones of his trumpet; the trusty king

the sound of his trumpet; the trusty king

had followed their trail with faithful band.

had followed after them with a faithful band.

~*~

Section XXXIX

"THE bloody swath of Swedes and Geats

"THE bloody expanse of Swedes and Geats

and the storm of their strife, were seen afar,

and the cruelty of their conflict, was seen from far away,

how folk against folk the fight had wakened.

how people against people had been drawn into the fight.

The ancient king with his atheling band

The ancient king with his band of warriors

sought his citadel, sorrowing much:

returned to his castle, with much sorrow:

Ongentheow earl went up to his burg.

Ongentheow the noble went back to his city.

He had tested Hygelac's hardihood,

He had tested Hygelac's hardiness,

the proud one's prowess, would prove it no longer,

the proud one's skill, would test it no longer,

defied no more those fighting-wanderers

defied no more those wandering fighters

nor hoped from the seamen to save his hoard,

and did not hope for the sailors to save his hoard,

his bairn and his bride: so he bent him again,
his child and his wife; so he returned again,

old, to his earth-walls. Yet after him came
old, to his fortress. Yet after him came

with slaughter for Swedes the standards of Hygelac
with slaughter for Swedes the flags of Hygelac

o'er peaceful plains in pride advancing,
over peaceful plains advancing proudly,

till Hrethelings fought in the fenced town.
until Hrethelings fought in the fenced town.

Then Ongentheow with edge of sword,
Then Ongentheow with the edge of a sword,

the hoary-bearded, was held at bay,
the thick-bearded, was held at bay,

and the folk-king there was forced to suffer
and the king of the people was forced to endure

Eofor's anger. In ire, at the king
Eofor's anger. In his wrath, at the king

Wulf Wonreding with weapon struck;

Wulf Wonreding struck with a weapon;

and the chieftain's blood, for that blow, in streams

and the chief's blood, for that blow, flowed in streams

flowed 'neath his hair. No fear felt he,

from beneath his hair. He felt no fear,

stout old Scylfing, but straightway repaid

sturdy old Scylfing, but paid him back straightaway

in better bargain that bitter stroke

in a batter bargain that terrible stroke

and faced his foe with fell intent.

and faced his foe with dark intentions.

Nor swift enough was the son of Wonred

The son of Wonred did not quickly enough

answer to render the aged chief;

reply in kind to the aged chief;

too soon on his head the helm was cloven;

the helm was cut in two too soon on his head;

blood-bedecked he bowed to earth,

he sank to the ground, covered in blood,

and fell adown; not doomed was he yet,

and fell down; but he was not doomed yet,

and well he waxed, though the wound was sore.

and started to recover, though the wound was bad.

Then the hardy Hygelac-thane,

Then the hardy king Hygelac,

when his brother fell, with broad brand smote,

when his brother fell, with a broad sword struck,

giants' sword crashing through giants'-helm

the giants' sword crashing through the giants' helmet

across the shield-wall: sank the king,

across the shield-wall: the king sank,

his folk's old herdsman, fatally hurt.

his people's old shepherd, fatally hurt.

There were many to bind the brother's wounds

There were many to bandage the brother's wounds

and lift him, fast as fate allowed

and lift him, as fast as they could

his people to wield the place-of-war.

his people to take back the battlefield.

But Eofor took from Ongentheow,

But Eofor took from Ongentheow,

earl from other, the iron-breastplate,

one noble from the other, the iron breastplate,

hard sword hilted, and helmet too,

the hard sword, and his helmet too,

and the hoar-chief's harness to Hygelac carried,

and the sturdy chief's armor he carried to Hygelac,

who took the trappings, and truly promised

who took the items, and truthfully promised

rich fee 'mid folk, -- and fulfilled it so.

a rich reward among the people, -- and indeed fulfilled it.

For that grim strife gave the Geatish lord,

For that grim conflict the Geatish lord

Hrethel's offspring, when home he came,

Hrethel's offspring, he came home,

to Eofor and Wulf a wealth of treasure.

a wealth of treasure of Eofor and Wulf.

Each of them had a hundred thousand

Each of them had a hundred thousand

in land and linked rings; nor at less price reckoned

in land and linked rings; they did not consider it less valuable

mid-earth men such mighty deeds!

men of that time, such mighty deeds!

And to Eofor he gave his only daughter

And gave to Eofor's only daughter

in pledge of grace, the pride of his home.

in a graceful pledge, a place in his proud home.

"Such is the feud, the foeman's rage,

"Such is the feud, the anger of the foe,

death-hate of men: so I deem it sure

the death-hate of men: so I think it certain

that the Swedish folk will seek us home

that the Swedish people will follow us home

for this fall of their friends, the fighting-Scylfings,

for this death of their friends, the fighting-Scylfings,

when once they learn that our warrior leader

the moment they learn that our warrior leader

lifeless lies, who land and hoard

lies lifeless, who always defended land and hoard

ever defended from all his foes,

from all his enemies,

furthered his folk's weal, finished his course

furthered his people's interests, finished his life

a hardy hero. -- Now haste is best,

a hardy hero. – Now it would be best that we quickly

that we go to gaze on our Geatish lord,

go to gaze on our Geatish lord,

and bear the bountiful breaker-of-rings

and take the generous gift-giver

to the funeral pyre. No fragments merely

to the funeral pyre. No mere fragments

shall burn with the warrior. Wealth of jewels,

shall burn with the warrior. The full wealth of jewels,

gold untold and gained in terror,

uncountable gold, gained in terror,

treasure at last with his life obtained,

the treasure he obtained with the last of his life,

all of that booty the brands shall take,

all of that treasure the weapons shall take,

fire shall eat it. No earl must carry

fire shall eat it. No noble can carry

memorial jewel. No maiden fair

a memorial jewel. No beautiful maiden

shall wreathe her neck with noble ring:

shall decorate her neck with a noble ring:

nay, sad in spirit and shorn of her gold,

no, sad in spirit and her gold taken from her,

oft shall she pass o'er paths of exile

often she shall pass over paths of exile

now our lord all laughter has laid aside,

now our lord has laid all laughter aside,

all mirth and revel. Many a spear

all cheer and celebration. Many a spear

morning-cold shall be clasped amain,

morning-cold shall be clasped again,

lifted aloft; nor shall lilt of harp

lifted aloft; and no sweet sound of the harp

those warriors wake; but the wan-hued raven,

wake those warriors; but the dark-colored raven,

fain o'er the fallen, his feast shall praise

standing over the fallen, shall praise in his feast

and boast to the eagle how bravely he ate

and brag to the eagle how bravely he ate

when he and the wolf were wasting the slain.

when he and the wolf were consuming the killed.

So he told his sorrowful tidings,

So he told his sad news,

and little he lied, the loyal man

and told no lies, the loyal man

of word or of work. The warriors rose;

of words or of actions. The warriors rose;

sad, they climbed to the Cliff-of-Eagles,

sadly, they climbed to the Cliff-of-Eagles,

went, welling with tears, the wonder to view.

went, filling up with tears, to see the sight.

Found on the sand there, stretched at rest,

They found on the sand there, stretched at rest,

their lifeless lord, who had lavished rings

their lifeless lord, who had so often given gifts

of old upon them. Ending-day

of old upon them. The last day

had dawned on the doughty-one; death had seized

had come to the enduring one; death had seized

in woful slaughter the Weders' king.

in woeful slaughter the Weders' king.

There saw they, besides, the strangest being,

They saw there, as well, the strangest being,

loathsome, lying their leader near,

disgusting, lying near their leader,

prone on the field. The fiery dragon,

limp on the field. The fiery dragon,

fearful fiend, with flame was scorched.

the fearful fiend, was scorched with flame.

Reckoned by feet, it was fifty measures

Measuring in feet, it was fifty

in length as it lay. Aloft erewhile

in length as it lay. Aloft, not long ago,

it had revelled by night, and anon come back,

it had enjoyed itself by night, and then come back,

seeking its den; now in death's sure clutch

seeking its den; now in death's certain grasp

it had come to the end of its earth-hall joys.

it had come to the end of its underground cavern's joys.

By it there stood the stoups and jars;

The jars and stoups stood by it there;

dishes lay there, and dear-decked swords

dishes lay there, and expensively decorated swords,

eaten with rust, as, on earth's lap resting,

eaten with rust, as, resting on the earth's lap,

a thousand winters they waited there.

they had waited there for a thousand years.

For all that heritage huge, that gold

For all that long heritage, that gold

of bygone men, was bound by a spell,

of men from the past, was bound by a spell

so the treasure-hall could be touched by none

so the treasure hall could not be touched by any

of human kind, -- save that Heaven's King,

human being, -- except if Heaven's King,

God himself, might give whom he would,

God himself, might allow whom he wished,

Helper of Heroes, the hoard to open, --

Helper of Heroes, to open the hoard, --

even such a man as seemed to him meet.

even such a man as seemed to him suitable.

~*~

Section XL

A PERILOUS path, it proved, he trod

A PERILOUS path, it turned out, he walked

who heinously hid, that hall within,

who sinfully hid, inside that hall,

wealth under wall! Its watcher had killed

the wealth underground! Its watcher had killed

one of a few, and the feud was avenged

a man like few men, and the feud was avenged

in woful fashion. Wondrous seems it,

in a woeful fashion. It seems puzzling

what manner a man of might and valor

what way a man of power and courage

oft ends his life, when the earl no longer

often ends his life, when the nobleman no longer

in mead-hall may live with loving friends.

may live in a mead-hall with loving friends.

So Beowulf, when that barrow's warden

So Beowulf, then he went to that barrow's guard

he sought, and the struggle; himself knew not

and the struggle; he himself did not know

in what wise he should wend from the world at last.

in what way he would leave the world at last.

For princes potent, who placed the gold,

For powerful princes, who placed the goal,

with a curse to doomsday covered it deep,

with a curse until the end of time covered it deep,

so that marked with sin the man should be,

so that a man would be marked with sin,

hedged with horrors, in hell-bonds fast,

his life full of horrors, held in hell-bonds,

racked with plagues, who should rob their hoard.

persecuted with plagues, who robbed their hoard.

Yet no greed for gold, but the grace of heaven,

Yet it was no greed for gold, but the grace of heaven,

ever the king had kept in view.

that the king had always kept in view.

Wiglaf spake, the son of Weohstan: --

Wiglaf spoke, the son of Weohstan: --

"At the mandate of one, oft warriors many

"At the command of one, often many warriors

sorrow must suffer; and so must we.

must suffer; and so must we.

The people's-shepherd showed not aught

The people's shepherd showed not the slightest

of care for our counsel, king beloved!

interest in our advice, beloved king!

That guardian of gold he should grapple not, urged we,

We urged him not to fight that guardian of gold,

but let him lie where he long had been

but let him lie where he had been for so long

in his earth-hall waiting the end of the world,

in his earth-hall awaiting the end of the world,

the hest of heaven. -- This hoard is ours

the command of heaven. – This hoard is ours

but grievously gotten; too grim the fate

but bought with too high a price; too grim the fate

which thither carried our king and lord.

which carried our king and lord there.

I was within there, and all I viewed,
I was inside, and I saw all,

the chambered treasure, when chance allowed me
the buried treasure, when chance allowed me

(and my path was made in no pleasant wise)
(and my path was not at all pleasant)

under the earth-wall. Eager, I seized
under the earth-wall. I eagerly seized

such heap from the hoard as hands could bear
such portions from the hoard as my hands could bear

and hurriedly carried it hither back
and hurriedly carried it here back

to my liege and lord. Alive was he still,
to my liege and lord. He was still alive,

still wielding his wits. The wise old man
still aware of himself. The wise old man

spake much in his sorrow, and sent you greetings
spoke much in his sorrow, and sent you greetings

and bade that ye build, when he breathed no more,

and told you to build, when he breathed no bore,

on the place of his balefire a barrow high,

on the place of his funeral fire a high barrow,

memorial mighty. Of men was he

a mighty memorial. Of men, he was

'

worthiest warrior wide earth o'er

the worthiest warrior over the wide earth

the while he had joy of his jewels and burg.

during the time he had joy of his jewels and city.

Let us set out in haste now, the second time

Let us hurry now, for a second time

to see and search this store of treasure,

to see and search in this store of treasure,

these wall-hid wonders, -- the way I show you, --

these hidden wonders, -- I will show you the way, --

where, gathered near, ye may gaze your fill

where, gathered near, you may gaze your fill

at broad-gold and rings. Let the bier, soon made,

at the broad gold and rings. Let the stretcher, soon made, be all in order when out we come,

be all ready when we come out,

our king and captain to carry thither

our king and captain to carry there

-- man beloved -- where long he shall bide

-- beloved man – where he shall stay long

safe in the shelter of sovran God."

safe in the shelter of sovereign God."

Then the bairn of Weohstan bade command,

Then the son of Weohstan commanded,

hardy chief, to heroes many

the hardy chief, to many heroes

that owned their homesteads, hither to bring

that owned their homesteads, to bring here

firewood from far -- o'er the folk they ruled –

firewood from far – over the people they ruled –

for the famed-one's funeral. "Fire shall devour

for the famous one's funeral. "Fire shall devour

featly feathered," followed the barb.

the hard-one treasure," followed the stinging command.

And now the sage young son of Weohstan

And now the wise young son of Weohstan

seven chose of the chieftain's thanes,

chose seven of the chieftain's men,

.

the best he found that band within,

the best he found within that band,

and went with these warriors, one of eight,

and went with these warriors, one of eight men,

under hostile roof. In hand one bore

under the hostile roof. In his hand one carried

a lighted torch and led the way.

a lighted torch and led the way.

No lots they cast for keeping the hoard

They did not divide up the hoard to keep

when once the warriors saw it in hall,

when the warriors saw it in the hall,

altogether without a guardian,

entirely without a guardian,

lying there lost. And little they mourned

lying there lost. And they did not mourn

when they had hastily haled it out,

when they quickly hauled it out,

dear-bought treasure! The dragon they cast,

the dearly-bought treasure! The dragon they threw

the worm, o'er the wall for the wave to take,

over the wall for the sea to take

and surges swallowed that shepherd of gems.

and waves swallowed that guardian of gems.

Then the woven gold on a wain was laden –

Then the woven gold was placed in a container –

countless quite! -- and the king was borne

quite countless! – and the king was carried

hoary hero, to Hrones-Ness.

the sturdy hero, to Hrones-Ness.

~*~

Section XLI

THEN fashioned for him the folk of Geats

THEN they made for him, the people of Geats,

firm on the earth a funeral-pile,

firmly on the earth a funeral-pile,

and hung it with helmets and harness of war

and hung it with helmets and armor of war

and breastplates bright, as the boon he asked;

and bright breastplates, as the favor he asked;

and they laid amid it the mighty chieftain,

and they placed among it the mighty chieftain,

heroes mourning their master dear.

heroes mourning their dear master.

Then on the hill that hugest of balefires

Then on the hill that hugest of funeral fires

the warriors wakened. Wood-smoke rose

the warriors lit. Wood-smoke rose

black over blaze, and blent was the roar

black over blaze, and blended was the roar

of flame with weeping (the wind was still),

of flame with weeping, since the wind was still,

till the fire had broken the frame of bones,

until the fire had broken the frame of bones,

hot at the heart. In heavy mood

hot at the heart. In a mournful mood

their misery moaned they, their master's death.

they moaned their misery, their master's death.

Wailing her woe, the widow old,

Crying her sadness, the old widow,

her hair upbound, for Beowulf's death

her hair knotted, for Beowulf's death

sung in her sorrow, and said full oft

sang in her sorrow, and often said

she dreaded the doleful days to come,

she dreaded the terrible days do come,

deaths enow, and doom of battle,

more deaths, and the doom of battle,

and shame. -- The smoke by the sky was devoured.

and shame. The sky devoured the smoke.

The folk of the Weders fashioned there

The Weder people made there

on the headland a barrow broad and high,

on the headland a broad and high barrow,

by ocean-farers far descried:

within sight of ocean-travelers far-off:

in ten days' time their toil had raised it,

in ten days' time their work raised it,

the battle-brave's beacon. Round brands of the pyre

the brave-in-battle's beacon. Around the edges of the pyre

a wall they built, the worthiest ever

they build a wall, the best ever

that wit could prompt in their wisest men.

that intelligence could bring from their wisest men.

They placed in the barrow that precious booty,

They placed in the barrow that precious treasure

the rounds and the rings they had reft erewhile,

the rounds and the rings they had taken earlier,

hardy heroes, from hoard in cave, --

hardy heroes, from the dragon's hoard in the cave, -

trusting the ground with treasure of earls,

trusting the ground with the treasure of nobles,

gold in the earth, where ever it lies

gold in the dirt, where it lies forever

useless to men as of yore it was.

as useless to men as it was in the past.

Then about that barrow the battle-keen rode,

Then around that barrow the battle-eager rode,

atheling-born, a band of twelve,

warrior-born, a band of twelve,

lament to make, to mourn their king,

to lament, to mourn their king,

chant their dirge, and their chieftain honor.

to chant their dirge, and speak of their chief's honor.

They praised his earlship, his acts of prowess

They praised his nobility, his acts of skill

worthily witnessed: and well it is

worthily witnessed: and it is good

that men their master-friend mightily laud,

that men mightily praise their master and friend,

heartily love, when hence he goes

deeply love, when he goes

from life in the body forlorn away.

from life and his body forlorn away.

Thus made their mourning the men of Geatland,

In this way mourned the men of Geatland,

for their hero's passing his hearth-companions:

for their hero's death his friends

quoth that of all the kings of earth,

said that of all the kings of earth,

of men he was mildest and most beloved,

of men he was the gentlest and most beloved,

to his kin the kindest, keenest for praise.

to his kin the kindest, most eager for praise.

Themes

Heroism

At its root, Beowulf is a story about a hero. But not just that, Beowulf embodies many heroic ideals commonly found in the middle ages, centering on bravery, strength, and honor. Beowulf is inhuman in his strength, but he is wise and just as well. He does not get in unnecessary fights or purposefully pick on those less strong than he is; instead he uses his strength to defend those weaker than himself. Heroes such as Beowulf are very common in legends and myths, and they adhere to a strict code of honor. In this sense, Beowulf is a very typical hero of ancient culture.

Kings and Lineage

In the feudal era, kings were of utmost importance to society. They won their positions by being the strongest warrior in the land. An ideal king was strong and would be able to protect their people from other violent influences and wars. In Beowulf, the first great warrior king of Denmark was Scyld, and from him many generations of kings were born. Lineage was very important to everybody, and many knew others not only by their name but by their father's name as well. Beowulf's father, for instance, although already deceased by the time the poem begins, is repeatedly brought up in conversation and his good reputation is added to Beowulf's.

Monsters

In Beowulf's world, monsters threatening the peace of humanity abound. Monsters serve as a way for heroes to show their strength and gain a reputation by slaying as many strong monsters as possible. The poem is divided up into three major fights in which Beowulf faces Grendel, Grendel's mother, and finally a terrifying dragon. According to the narrator, Grendel and his mother are both descendants of Cain along with all the monsters in the rest of the world. In this perspective, these fictional monsters represent the twisted and warped parts humanity that the heroes must fight against.

Weapons

What would a hero be without a legendary weapon? In Beowulf, special attention is given to impressive weapons, especially swords. During his second fight with Grendel's mother, another warrior named Unferth lends Beowulf his family sword, passed down through the generations. Later, Beowulf finds a legendary sword used by giants that was said never to have lost a battle. The weapons, it seems, have just as much to their reputation as the heroes who wield them. Although Beowulf proves that he is a hero without the use of a weapon when he faces Grendel completely unarmed in order to gain more glory.

Treasure

One of the benefits of going around slaying monsters was acquiring rare and ancient treasures. Either taken from the monster's lair or given as payment, treasure was a very important aspect of Beowulf's story. Beowulf is rewarded with great treasures for defeating both Grendel and his mother. However, he does not keep the treasure for himself but gives it freely to his kinsman Hygelac. Valuable treasures were passed down in families and served as important heirlooms in society. After Beowulf slew the dragon, he was thankful that he would leave so much treasure for his people as his legacy. In many respects, the value of treasure was not in the gold and jewels but rather in reputation and history.

Paganism

Although the narrator of Beowulf is Christian, there is still a definite influence of paganism throughout the stories in the poem. When Hrothgar and his people become terrorized by Grendel, the wise men convene and send offering to the gods in order to appease them. Even Grendel and the other monsters have roots in ancient pagan culture, although a Christian spin is put on them by explaining them as the descendants of Cain. The culture of heroes and slaying monsters is definitely from the old world of Scandinavia.

Christianity

Although the original myths did not include Christian influences, the anonymous writer who penned the poem added Christianity throughout the legends. The characters themselves rarely mention The Lord or refer to the Christian religion; the narrator, however, frequently interjects with observations about the actions and motivations of the characters, painting them in a good or bad light based on how much they coincide with Christian morals and values. There are many points where the Christian narrator seems to struggle with equating the old stories with the new way of looking at the world.

Gender

The middle ages were a time of very strict gender roles. Men took the role of powerful protector, and women gentle housekeepers. The poem touches on the issue of gender briefly by comparing Hygelac's queen, Hygd, with an ancient queen who was arrogant and violent. The narrator makes it clear that the ideal woman is gentle, beautiful and wise. The most interesting case in Beowulf is Grendel's mother, a swamp demon who has lost all semblance of femininity and is considered a warped being. She takes on a very active, masculine role in avenging her son and is eventually punished for it by Beowulf.

Water

In Beowulf, water is the symbol of ancient and unknown things. Both Grendel and his mother came from the swamp, which is reminiscent of the primordial waters in ancient creation myths. Hrothgar warns Beowulf that the bottom of the swamp waters has never been explored. Beowulf, being the hero, makes it down to the bottom while fighting off numerous sea monsters. Under water, he does not have his full strength and it is almost as if the water weakens him. Later, when the dragon dies, the warriors push its body off a cliff and into the water below.

Light

Just as water signifies ancient places and darkness, light continually acts throughout the poem as a signifier of God and heroism. When Beowulf kills Grendel's mother, a light shines out through the dark waters allowing Beowulf to find Grendel's body. The narrator makes many references to God being associated with light, and monsters with darkness. Even the dragon dwells in a vast underground cave and only after it is defeated can the warriors explore the cavern using torches and golden banners to light their way.

Characters

Beowulf

The protagonist and namesake of the poem, Beowulf is a man of great power who seeks glory by slaying monsters and helping others. He is from Geatland, and comes from a noble family. He seeks honor and glory at the risk of his own life, as shown when he decided to face Grendel without weapons or armor so that it would be an even match. Eventually Beowulf became king of the Geats, and was loved by all. He gave his life slaying the dragon that was terrorizing his country and was revered after his death.

Narrator

While the narrator of Beowulf is not named nor does he ever appear, his writing sets the stage for all the action to take place, and his comments frame how the reader is supposed to think about the events and the characters. Originally, the legends of Beowulf had no Christian influences, but since the narrator is writing the poem from a Christian standpoint he adds to the poem to create a bridge between the old and new cultures of the Anglo-Saxon people.

Hrothgar

The elderly warrior king of Denmark, Hrothgar is descended from a long line of warrior kings. He built the great mead hall named Heorot as a symbol of his peaceful and prosperous reign. Even in his old age, Hrothgar was well respected by his people and he was crushed when Grendel began terrorizing not only Heorot by the rest of the country as well. When Beowulf successfully defeats Grendel and his mother, Hrothgar shows all the necessary courtesy and treats Beowulf as his own son.

Healhtheow

Hrothgar's queen, Healhtheow joins him at all the important feasts. She wears a large amount of gold jewelry, and, fittingly, awarded Beowulf with several of the more valuable treasures for killing the monsters that threatened Denmark. In Heorot, Healhtheow was the picture of the perfect hostess and acted kindly towards Beowulf and his warriors.

Unferth

A Dane warrior who is envious of Beowulf's fame throughout the country. The night before Beowulf faces Grendel, Unferth tries to mock him by saying that he is not as strong as he needs to be to defeat Grendel and that he lost a swimming match to his friend Breca when they were young. Beowulf counters these insults with his version of events in which he slew hundreds of sea monsters during the swim and still beat Breca, winning the confidence of the Danes. Later, Unferth apologizes and even lends Beowulf his family sword in recompense.

Grendel

Grendel is an evil descendant of Cain who lives in the swamp near the great hall of Heorot. He heard the Danes' merrymaking and became angry, slaughtering thirty men the first night and continuing his rampage for over a decade. Grendel has no reason to be evil other than he was born of a traitor and a murderer. Many scholars believe that he symbolizes the original evil in mankind because he seems to be part human and part monster. During his fight with Beowulf, Grendel has his shoulder and arm torn off by Beowulf and flees to the swamp to die.

Grendel's Mother

Like Grendel, Grendel's mother is also an evil descendant of Cain. She comes out of the swamp after her son is killed seeking revenge on those who hurt him. While she is just as vicious as her son, she is not as strong and is forced to flee Heorot after only killing one person. Beowulf chases her underwater, and after a battle in which he is almost killed himself, slays her with a giant's sword. When she is dead, a light appears and all the sea monsters are gone from the waters. Like Grendel, she symbolizes the abstract evil present in man.

Hygelac

The king of Geatland and one of Beowulf's few kinsmen, Hygelac is an honorable and well-loved king in the poem. Although he only appears for one scene, he and Beowulf appear to be very close. He is greatly relieved to see Beowulf safe after defeating Grendel. Beowulf, being loyal to both kinsman and king, gives all the treasure he earned from his adventures to Hygelac, who in turn rewards Beowulf with lands and riches.

Hygd

Hygd is Hygelac queen, hailed for her gentleness and beauty. She is contrasted in the poem to an ancient queen who frequently had people killed just for looking at her in a way she didn't like. Hygd is nothing like this, and is praised for embodying the gentle feminine standards of the Anglo-Saxon culture.

The Dragon

The third and final monster that Beowulf faces, the dragon is an ancient creature who was cursed to horde treasure found in graves. He finds a vast cavern full of treasure amassed by a man who was the last of his clan. The dragon guarded the cave for three hundred years until a servant accidentally found the cave and ran out with a golden goblet. The dragon ravaged the countryside, eventually burning down Beowulf's throne and forcing him to fight. Unlike Grendel and his mother, the dragon does not have any sort of humanity about it, and is killed unceremoniously. For killing the dragon, Beowulf is compared to the greatest hero of all time, who also killed a dragon.

Wiglaf

Wiglaf is a young Geatish warrior who helps Beowulf defeat the dragon when all the others run towards the woods in fear of the beast. Wiglaf has a strong sense of honor and courage and reprimands the other warriors, calling them cowards for running away. He is with Beowulf at the very end, and before the hero dies he gives the young warrior his armor. At the end of the poem, Wiglaf seems like the most likely successor of Beowulf since he has no heirs.

Chapter Summary

Prelude

Beowulf opens hailing the great warrior kings of Danes. The first of these kings was named Scyld the Scefing. Although he was abandoned by his parents, he was very strong and soon rose to power. When he became king, his subjects showered him with gifts and honor. Soon, Scyld had an heir, a boy named Beow. He became famous and earned the loyalty of all his father's clansmen.

Sadly, Scyld died in battle before he reached old age, and requested to be returned to the ocean. His people loaded a ship with all sorts of treasures, armor and weapons and placed him on it. They hoisted a gold banner before sending the ship out to the ocean, as Scyld had wanted. The people grieved deeply at their king's passing.

I

Beow, having already become well-known and well-loved, became king after his father passed away. Eventually, his heir Halfdane succeeded him. Halfdane had a reputation for being a wise man, and was blessed with four children. He had three sons, Heorogar, Hrothgar and Halga, as well as one daughter who became the Queen of Swedes.

Hrothgar was a glorified warrior, and soon became famous throughout the land. He decided to build a great hall from which to rule from, and brought builders from all over the world to construct it. When it was completed, Hrothgar named the hall Heorot. Here Hrothgar ruled, as well as distributed gifts and drank with his men.

The clansmen lived in a time of peace, and enjoyed many years of drinking and merry making. However, that peace ended when Grendel, a descendant of Cain, came out of the swamp. Grendel was banished to exile by the creator, and spent his life among the other evil descendants of Cain. These included bad spirits, elves and giants. Despite the fact that they would never win, these evil forces continually battled against the Creator.

II

One night Grendel came out of the swamp and listened to the revelers singing and partying. After they fell asleep, he went inside the great hall and slaughtered thirty of the men before going back to his lair. At dawn, the men awoke and realized that there had been a massacre in the night. The people began mourning, and the leader of the Danes trailed Grendel back to his lair. They did not find him, however, and the next night Grendel struck again.

Eventually the great hall stood empty. For twelve years Grendel terrorized the country, bringing sorrow wherever he went. The people began spreading tales about how Grendel's hatred for Hrothgar and his people. Grendel refused to make peace with the men, and could not be bought with gold. He preyed on the young and old alike, and everyone was terrified of him.

Hrothgar was grief-stricken because he could not hold Heorot. He brought together the nobles of the land and any wise men he could find to see if they had any ideas. However, nothing could be done and they made offerings to the pagan gods because they did not have any ideas. The narrator points out that they did not know they could ask for help from The Lord.

III

Eventually, the tales of Grendel spread to surrounding countries. Beowulf, a relative of Hygelac, was the greatest warrior of the Geats. When he heard of Grendel, he decided to help Hrothgar. Although he was loved by his people, they let him leave and blessed him. Beowulf chose fourteen of the boldest men in the kingdom and prepared for the journey. The fourteen warriors, fully armed with mail and weapons, boarded a ship to cross the sea. They sailed to Hrothgar's land, and eventually landed safely. They climbed ashore and prayed to the gods, thanking them for safe passage.

A Scylding clansman, watching from a cliff, saw the warriors come ashore. He saw their glittering armor and weapons, and wondered what kind of men they were. Immediately, he got on his horse and rode down to find out. When he got closer, he pointed his spear at them and began asking questions. Although he noticed that one of the warriors looked like a great hero, he was still suspicious because they might be spies. He threatens them to speak quickly and tell him why they have come ashore.

IV

The leader of the warriors begins to speak, answering the clansman's questions. He explains that they are from the clan of Geats, and that his father's name is Extheow. They heard of the terror that has been wrecked on Hrothgar and have come to help slay the monster once and for all.

After hearing their story, the clansmen happily grants the warriors passage across the land. He promises to send men to guard their boat while they are trying to kill Grendel so that they can return home safely. The clansman shows them the way to Heorot, and eventually they come to the great hall, which is the most beautiful building in sight. The clansman leaves the warriors, wishing them luck before he returns to guard their ship.

V

When Beowulf and his men get to the great hall, they set down their weapons and armor to rest. A warrior of Hrothgar approaches them and asks who they are, remarking that he has never seen men with so much armor before. Beowulf greets the warrior, giving him name and asking to speak to Hrothgar himself. The warrior tells them to wait while he asks Hrothgar if he will see them.

The warrior goes to where Hrothgar sits, still surrounded by his men though he is now old and gray. He gives Hrothgar the news that there is a group of warriors who wish to talk to him, and advises Hrothgar to listen to them because their leader looks like a mighty hero.

VI

Hrothgar tells Wulfgar, his warrior, to welcome the group in. Hrothgar knew Beowulf's father, and has heard tales of Beowulf's legendary strength. He is glad that such brave men have come to help him in his time of need, and intends to welcome them as honored guests. Wulfgar travels back to the band of warriors with his message of welcome from Hrothgar. He says that they will be allowed inside Heorot in their armor, but insists that they leave their weapons outside. Beowulf and his warriors leave their weapons, and a few men stay behind to guard them.

Inside, Beowulf greets Hrothgar very formally. He goes into detail about some of his famed battles, and asks Hrothgar for permission to kill Grendel. Beowulf wishes to fight Grendel in single combat, and since Grendel does not use weapons Beowulf does not intend to either. He vows to either kill Grendel or be killed himself. Beowulf does have one request though, and that is in the event of his death that Hrothgar send his armor back to his land since his body will be eaten by the monster.

VII

Hrothgar responds to Beowulf's request by recalling the actions of his father, who killed Heatholaf of the Wylfings and sailed to Hrothgar who had become the ruler of the Danes not long before. Hrothgar settled the argument by sending a tribute to the Wylfings, and after that Ecgtheow swore his loyalty to Hrothgar.

Although Hrothgar does not wish to ask others for help in solving his problems, the situation with Grendel has become so desperate that he has no choice. He tells Beowulf that he may fight Grendel, but warns him that many other brave warriors have come to Heorot vowing that they would kill the famed monster. None of them succeeded and are now dead. Nevertheless, he invites Beowulf and his men to sit down and feast with them.

VIII

A man named Unferth spoke up during the feast. He was envious of Beowulf's achievements, and tries to undermine him. He asks Beowulf if he is the same man who swam across the ocean despite great risk to himself and lost to Brecaa. Even though they fought for seven days, Unferth mocks that no one has lasted one day against Grendel despite their bravery.

Beowulf calmly replies to Unferth with his own version of the story. He tells Unferth that he must have drank too much beer and not remembered right. Both boys, he and Breca decided to swim the ocean. They took weapons to defend themselves, and set out. They swam for five days before a huge storm overtook them. Sea monsters were awakened, and one of them dragged Beowulf down to the deeps before Beowulf managed to kill it with his sword. Monsters continued attacking, but Beowulf killed them.

IX

By the end of the night, the shores were safe and no sailors ever had trouble in those waters a gain. Beowulf came to shore unhurt but exhausted. He takes a break from his story to mock Unferth, saying that he has never fought a battle like that, and also pointing out that if he were as brave as he talked, Grendel wouldn't be going around terrorizing the Danes. Although many brave men have died trying to defeat Grendel, Beowulf is confident that he will be victorious.

After hearing this tale, Hrothgar and his hall became joyous. The Queen comes out with a cup and gives it to Hrothgar to drink. After he drinks, she takes the cup to everyone in the hall before stopping at Beowulf. As he takes the cup, Beowulf gives a short, formal speech, reiterating his confidence. The Queen sits down next to her husband and the feast continues.

When the sun sinks down below the horizon, Hrothgar and his men leave. Hrothgar remarks that Beowulf's group is the first he has ever left in the hall alone, and promises that if they defeat Grendel that they can ask for anything they want within his power.

X

Hrothgar and his men leave the hall for the night. Beowulf casts off his armor and sets aside his weapons. He gives a speech to his men, reminding them of why he is going to fight Grendel with armor, sword or shield. Beowulf then asks God to grant the victory to whoever is in the right. After his speech, Beowulf relaxes while his men lie awake in bed. None of them know for sure if they will go back home. In the dark, Grendel makes his way towards the great hall.

XI

Grendel makes his way to the great hall from the swamp. He sees the heroes, all asleep, and walks in with eyes aflame. He laughs when he sees them sleeping, and thinks about how he will kill them all before sunrise. He grabs the warrior closest to him and kills him, drinking his blood and eating his body piece by piece until there is nothing left. After his feast, Grendel moves towards the great hero who is reclining thinking to take him next.

Beowulf has been awake the whole time, and has watched Grendel devour the warrior. Grendel thinks about leaving, but suddenly his fingers are caught by some enormous strength. Beowulf has ahold of Grendel's hand, and for Grendel is afraid. He thinks of his safe den back in the swamp, and breaks free trying to escape. Beowulf chases after him, and the hall awakens.

Everything is chaos; the warriors are awake, and some of the Danes have come back. They see Beowulf fighting Grendel, and are amazed at the destruction that the two inflict on the hall. They are surprised that it is able to stand such an intense battle. Suddenly they hear a terrifying wail - Grendel is injured and Beowulf has him pinned.

XII

Beowulf and Grendel are still struggling in the hall, and the warriors around them try to help by striking at Grendel with their swords and spears. However, none of their weapons can pierce Grendel's skin because he is protected by a powerful spell. Despite this, Grendel begins to lose strength and gives in to Beowulf, whose grip on the demon is so strong that Grendel's very bones and muscles begin to give away. Finally, Beowulf succeeds in ripping the entire arm off Grendel, who knows he is going to die. Grendel is driven out of the hall and goes back to his lair in the swamp to die.

Beowulf has once again proven himself, and saved the Danes from the evil terror of Grendel. As proof of Beowulf's bravery, the shoulder and arm Beowulf ripped off of Grendel was mounted on the wall of the great hall.

XIII

In the morning people traveled from all around to the hall in order to see proof of Beowulf's victory and to celebrate. They looked at the footprints Grendel left as he fled the hall and followed them all the way to the demon's lair in the swamp. In Grendel's den they found large amounts of blood, and also realized Grendel had drowned himself in the muddy waters. Sure that his soul was now in hell, the clansmen rode home from the swamp in a joyous mood.

Tales began to spread of Beowulf's glory, and he was hailed as the most valiant warrior in the world. However, the Danes remained loyal to Hrothgar, their king. Songs began to be sung about Beowulf, and he was likened to the legendary warrior Sigemund. During his life, Sigemund was famous for killing monsters but his crowning glory was killing a vicious dragon that had a horde of treasure. Sigemund slew the dragon with his sword and took the gold back to his kingdom.

Eventually, Hrothgar himself came to the hall in order to see the proof of Grendel's destructions, and brought his queen with him.

XIV

Hrothgar reached the hall and saw Grendel's arm on the wall. He is very grateful that Grendel is dead, and admits that he had lost all hope of Grendel ever being killed. Beowulf, however, succeeded in vanquishing the evil terror, and for that Hrothgar offers Beowulf any wealth in the kingdom. He goes even further, announcing to all the warriors and clansmen that he will think of Beowulf as one of his own sons from that day forth. He says that Beowulf's fame will spread throughout the world, and that his name will never be forgotten.

Beowulf responds to Hrothgar, telling him that he is happy to have killed such a terrible monster. The only thing he wished is that Grendel had died in the hall instead of escaping back to the swamp. Beowulf says that everything happened as God had planned, and that there is still the proof of Grendel's arm to satisfy the king.

Throughout the speeches, Unferth, who had mocked Beowulf earlier and tried to undermine his strength, remained silent. The arm Beowulf took from Grendel was hard, and the claws described as being made of steel. It was obvious that a sword could never have severed the arm from the rest of Grendel's body, and so the fact that Beowulf ripped it off is proof of Beowulf's enormous strength.

XV

The men and women gathered in the hall began to clean and repair it for the upcoming feast to be held in celebration of Grendel's death. The hall, however, was in bad shape from the fight. Only the roof was untouched by the fierce battle waged the night before. Eventually, the hall was ready for the feast and Hrothgar himself arrived to attend the banquet. Noble men from all over the land traveled to Heorot in order to celebrate with Beowulf and Hrothgar, and they drank merrily.

During the feast, Hrothgar bestowed many gifts upon Beowulf in payment of his mighty deed. He gave the warrior a new set of armor, a battle banner woven with gold and a splendid sword. Beowulf drank in the hall with everyone else, and he was not ashamed to be seen receiving such valuable gifts in front of his men because he knew he deserved them.

Hrothgar had his men lead in eight war horses. One of the horses had a saddle that was set with jewels; Hrothgar had used the saddle during his battle days, and gave it graciously to Beowulf along with the other gifts.

XVI

The Geats were also paid back in gold for the warrior that Grendel killed, and everyone admitted that if Beowulf had not been there that all the warriors would most likely have been killed by Grendel as well. The narrator remarks that through God, men are blessed with insight.

After this last gift, minstrels begin singing. One of Hrothgar's singers begins the tale of Finn and his sons. Finn was the ruler of the Frisians and his wife was named Hildeburh. She was also the sister of Hnaef, the ruler of the Danes. During a battle between the two warring tribes, Hnaef was killed along with Hildeburh's son. At these losses, and also the large amount of casualties on both sides of the battlefield, Hildeburh began to grieve.

A truce was offered, and the two sides made a treaty promising to treat each other fairly. Hnaef, a great warrior, was burned on a pyre beside Hildeburh's son. Hildeburh grieved over them both as they burned until their bodies were completely consumed by the flames.

XVII

Because it was winter, the Danes were forced to stay with Finn and his people until spring came. Although they kept the truce, the leader of the Danes, named Hengest, still harbored bad feelings towards Finn. When it came time for them to leave, they slaughtered Finn and his kinsman, taking his treasures and his wife back with them to Denmark.

The song is finished, and the Queen enters the hall, sitting next to her husband. It is noted that although Unferth did try to shame Beowulf that he still has a good reputation among the men because of his courage. The Queen speaks to Hrothgar, telling him that she supports him naming Beowulf one of their sons. She believes that when Hrothgar dies and her sons ascend the throne that Beowulf will be a friend to them when they need help. She looks over at Beowulf, who is sitting on the benches in between her sons Hrothric and Hrothmund.

XVIII

The Queen gives Beowulf a cup and gifts of gold and jewels. The pieces of jewelry she gifted Beowulf with were worn by other great men in the past, mighty warriors. When the hall erupts in talk and excitement about the gifts, the Queen tells everyone that Beowulf has earned them with his deeds. She says that Beowulf's name will never be forgotten, and prays that he will be blessed. She also asks that he be a friend to her children if they ever need him.

After her speech, the Queen returns to Hrothgar's side. When the feast is over, Hrothgar and his men leave to go to sleep. No one knows that a new danger is outside, waiting. The clansmen sleep with their weapons and shields nearby because they are always ready to protect their leader.

XIX

All those in the hall went to sleep. They did not know it, but another monster was coming to the hall - Grendel's mother. She had been banished to the swamps after Cain killed Abel. Cain became the father of all monsters, including her son Grendel whom Beowulf killed with the help of God. Now Grendel's mother, grieving over her son's death, comes to Heorot to avenge him.

She bursts into the hall with great strength, but because she is a woman her strength is a little less than Grendel's. The warriors in the hall wake up and Grendel's mother decides to flee. Before she goes, she grabs her son's arm as well as one of Hrothgar's liegemen and takes them back with her to the swamp. Beowulf was not in the hall to stop her because he was sleeping somewhere else that night.

Seeing the destruction caused by monsters, Hrothgar is saddened and laments that his grief will never come to an end. In the morning Beowulf comes into the hall, unaware of the attack the night before. He asks Hrothgar if he slept peacefully throughout the night.

XX

Hrothgar is offended that Beowulf dares to ask such a mindless question. Seeing that Beowulf does not know the night's events, Hrothgar tells him of the female monster who came to avenge Grendel. The man she took in the night was Hrothgar's advisor and one of his close friends, Aeschere.

Across the land there were tales of two monsters, one male and one female. The male was Grendel, and the one who attacked the great hall Hrothgar believes to be the female in the stories. The two monsters live in an extremely dangerous part of the swamp. It is so inhospitable that it has never been fully explored. The tales say that by night the water is lit on fire, and that all who have entered into the deep water there have never come out.

Despite this peril, Hrothgar asks Beowulf if he will once again be brave and come to the rescue of the Danes. If Beowulf is willing to follow the demon into the swamp and kill her, Hrothgar promises to give Beowulf large amounts of ancient treasure and gold.

XXI

Beowulf tells Hrothgar that he will gladly avenge the death of Aeschere. He remarks that everyone must die, but Beowulf plans on winning as much glory as he can before that happens. Beowulf vows to Hrothgar that he will track down Grendel's mother in the swamp, saying confidently that she will not be able to hide from him even if she decides to flee.

Beowulf has horses saddled and mounts on his own steed, leading his men off towards the swamp. They follow Grendel's mother's foot prints across the plain and the moor until they come to some cliffs. The waters at the bottom of the cliffs are dyed red with blood, and the men go to investigate. When they get to the shore, they are dismayed to see Aeschere's head floating on the waves.

Sea monsters are in the water, drawn to the scent of blood. The warriors sound their horns and the monsters begin swimming away. One of them is shot by the warden of Geats with his bow, and it begins to die in the water. The other warriors go over and finish it off with their spears, dragging it ashore when it is dead.

Beowulf appears, ready for battle. His armor is shining and he has his gold helmet on to protect him. In his hand is an ancient weapon called Hrunting. The sword was lent to him by none other than Unferth, who gave it to Beowulf after drinking at the feast.

XXII

Beowulf speaks to Hrothgar, reminding him that, if he should die in battle, to take care of his men and send his gifts back to his homeland. He then bequeaths his own sword to Unferth, in exchange for using the legendary Hrunting. With this, Beowulf says that he will either kill Grendel's mother or die trying before plunging into the water.

He swims most of a day before coming in sight of the bottom of the ocean. Grendel's mother realizes that she is being followed, and reaches out at him with her claws. Beowulf's armor, however, protects him from her attacks. Many sea monsters tried to kill Beowulf while he chases after the female demon, but he fends them off.

Eventually, Beowulf spots a hall which he guesses is Grendel's mother's lair. He sees her and swings Hrunting directly at her. Even though the sword has never lost a battle, it is incapable of piercing her flesh. Realizing that the sword is useless, Beowulf flings it aside in order that he can fight with his bare hands. Beowulf seizes her by the shoulder and she falls to the ground. Quickly she fights back, and the two grapple until Beowulf, spent, falls down. Grendel's mother takes a short sword and drives it at Beowulf in order to take her revenge. His armor once again protects him, and Beowulf is spared.

XXIII

After Beowulf stood, he saw the ancient sword of Eotens which, according to legend, was the most powerful sword in the world. It was made by giants and regular men could not swing it because it was so heavy. Beowulf, however, lifts the sword and, in one sweep, cuts off Grendel's mother's head. She sinks to the floor, the blade bloodied. After the demon is killed, a light blazes out. Curious, Beowulf looks around him to see if he can find the cause. As Beowulf walks down the hall, he spots Grendel's corpse. Angry at all the men Grendel had killed, Beowulf cuts off his head.

Above the waters, Hrothgar and the group see that large amounts of blood are turning the water red. It has been nine hours since Beowulf went into the water, and Hrothgar and his men give up hope of him returning. Beowulf's warriors, both fearing and hoping, wait to see if Beowulf will emerge from the depths.

Back under the water, Beowulf's sword is melting after touching Grendel's blood. The blade dissolves, leaving the massive jeweled hilt. Beowulf heads back up, noticing that since the demon has been killed all the sea monsters have disappeared. There are many treasures in the deep, but he takes only Grendel's head and the sword hilt as proof of his conquest.

Once at the surface, his men greet him gladly and thank God for his safe return. Grendel's head is so heavy that four men have to carry it back to Hrothgar's hall. When they enter the hall with Beowulf and the severed head everyone is amazed.

XXIV

Beowulf speaks to Hrothgar, announcing that he succeeded in killing Grendel's mother, and almost died in the process. However, he was shielded by the Lord. The great sword Hrunting did not do Beowulf any good, but he found an even greater weapon hanging on the wall. Although the blade itself disintegrated, Beowulf shows the king the hilt he brought back from the depths. He goes on to assure Hrothgar that his kingdom is now safe from both the evil demons, and gave him the hilt as a gift.

Hrothgar examines the hilt and is amazed at how old it is. The sword hilt is passed down through the generations, becoming a treasured heirloom that reminds the people of the trials they have overcome. Hrothgar speaks to Beowulf, telling him that he is grateful once again for saving the kingdom, and reiterates his promise to treat Beowulf as family. He calls Beowulf a true hero, and tells everyone that his name will pass into legend. Not only does Hrothgar consider Beowulf strong, but recognizes that he has wisdom as well. Hrothgar tells the story of the former king Heremod, who was a violent and unwise king, and warns Beowulf against ever becoming too proud.

XXV

Hrothgar continues his speech, telling Beowulf that he should not forget his own mortality. He is strong now, but one day he will be old and no longer invulnerable. Hrothgar himself believed in his youth that nothing could keep him from defending his people; the coming of Grendel got rid of those illusions. Hrothgar thanks Beowulf for killing both Grendel and his mother, telling him that in the morning he will receive his treasure.

He invites Beowulf and his warriors to sit and feast in celebration. Beowulf is glad to be able to sit down, and the banquet begins. After the feast, Beowulf goes to bed and everyone in the hall sleeps peacefully.

In the morning Beowulf and his warriors are getting ready to go home. Beowulf gives Hrunting back to Unferth, and even though it failed him in battle Beowulf still praises the sword and thanks Unferth for lending it to him. After graciously giving Unferth back his sword, Beowulf makes his way to Hrothgar.

XXVI

Beowulf speaks to Hrothgar, telling him that they plan to go back to Hygelac. He tells the king that if he ever has any more need of him to just call and Beowulf will come to his aid with thousands of warriors. He also says that if Hrothgar's son Hrethric ever comes to Geats that he will be treated as a friend.

Hrothgar answers him, telling Beowulf that he is wise beyond his years. He hopes that Beowulf will be a good leader, and expresses a genuine fondness for the young hero. Hrothgar declares that their two kingdoms will have a mutual peace, and will not hesitate to help the other in a time of need as long as he is alive. After the speech, Hrothgar presents Beowulf with twelve treasures to take back with him.

They bid farewell for a final time, and Hrothgar hugs Beowulf. Hrothgar has a feeling that he and Beowulf will not see each other again, and Hrothgar truly loves him as a son. After their farewell, Beowulf goes towards the boat.

XXVII

Beowulf and his men get to the shore, and greet the warden who was guarding their boat for them. They load the treasure and horses onto the ship, and Beowulf gives a golden sword to the man for faithfully guarding their boat. After loading up the ship, Beowulf and his warriors leave Daneland and travel back to Geatland. A guard was stationed on the cliffs of their homeland to watch for their return, and he comes to the beach to greet them. They bring the ship ashore, and he anchors it so that it will not blow away.

Beowulf asks the men to carry the treasure back home to where Hygelac dwells. Hygelac lives in a mighty castle and has a young queen named Hygd. She is a good queen, and is not prideful like the ancient queen who had men killed just for looking at her face. The ancient queen was named Modthyrth, but legend told that she became less cruel after marrying the mighty warrior Offa.

XXVIII

Beowulf goes quickly to Hygelac's castle, and Hygelac is told of the hero's return. After hearing the good news, Hygelac orders the hall to be made ready for Beowulf and his men, and when they arrive he greets them warmly. He offers them seats at his table, and wants to know everything that happened on their journey. He reminds Beowulf that he did not want him to undertake such a risky venture, but is glad that he is home safe.

Beowulf responds to Hygelac, telling him that he did succeed in killing Grendel and by doing so avenging all those he killed. He tells Hygelac that when he arrived at Hrothgar's hall he and his men were treated very well by both Hrothgar and his queen. During his stay, Beowulf overheard that Hrothgar's daughter is supposed to marry a prince of Heathobard, one of the Dane's former enemies. In the past, many battles were waged over land and there were many casualties on both sides. Beowulf is afraid that the marriage will bring the two clans too close and, being reminded of the wrongs done to the other, will start the fighting anew.

Realizing that he has gotten off track, Beowulf turns the tale back to Grendel. He tells Hygelac of how they waited for the monster in the great hall, and how he killed only one warrior before trying to ensnare Beowulf and getting caught. Beowulf is a good storyteller, and makes sure to make everything sound intense. He tells Hygelac that after Grendel was killed Hrothgar rewarded him handsomely and they feasted. That night Grendel's mother came and Beowulf was asked to follow her into the swamp to kill her in her lair. Beowulf tells Hygelac that he succeeded once again, and that Hrothgar rewarded him with even more treasure.

XXIX

Beowulf offers his kinsman and prince all the treasures that he received from Hrothgar. He knows that he does not have many remaining kinsman, and wishes to please his uncle. He gives Hygelac the suit of armour and ancient sword that was used by Heorogar, as well as four of the armoured horses. To Hygelac's wife Beowulf gifted three horses and a beautiful necklace. Beowulf was strong as well as wise, to treat his family so well. Even though Beowulf was stronger than most men, he did not commit violence needlessly or get into drunken brawls.

In return for his gifts Hygelac gives Beowulf an ancient heirloom sword of their family and lays it in his lap. He also gives him a large portion of land and a huge manor. After a few years Hygelac is killed, and his son cannot protect the kingdom. Beowulf becomes king of the realm, and rules for fifty years. After fifty years, Beowulf is old but wise, and a new danger presents itself. A Dragon lives in a nearby mountain range, and one day someone steals a golden goblet from its horde of treasure. Because of this crime, the dragon's wrath will be unleashed on all the people of Geatland.

XXX

The man who stole the goblet did not do so on purpose. He was fleeing from his master and sought shelter in the cave where the dragon lived. He saw the treasure, and then the dragon. Terrified, he ran out of the cave carrying the goblet that was in his hand.

The treasure belonged to an ancient lord, who hid all his possessions deep in the earth. He was the last of his people, and the treasure was his one pleasure. His people were killed in battle, and the ancient lord wished that the treasure would never be touched by another man. Eventually he died and a dragon found his treasure. This particular dragon was cursed to take treasure from graves and it stayed in that cave for three hundred years.

When the thief went back to his master and told them of the great treasure hidden beneath the ground, they decided to plunder it. When the dragon awoke, it was very angry and followed the men who stole its treasure. The dragon began to burn the country side, and eventually its wrath would cause Beowulf's end.

XXXI

The dragon continued to burn the land and people of Geatland, and eventually it even burned the throne room of the Geats - Beowulf's home. Beowulf, now old, becomes saddened at this tragedy. He thinks that it is his fault the dragon is terrorizing his kingdom and becomes bitter. Realizing that something must be done, Beowulf plots vengeance. He commands the welders to make an enormous war shield out of iron so that it cannot burn against the dragon's flames.

Beowulf knew that his life would end along with the dragon's. He did not fear the dragon, because even after he earned fame by killing Grendel and his mother he continued to fight many monsters and earn even more glory. He triumphed in the battle his kinsman Hygelac was killed in, and swam while wearing thirty coats of armour. After Hygelac was slain, Hygd welcomes Beowulf back to the kingdom and Hygelac's son took over the realm. However, he died in another fight against the enemies of the Geats, and Beowulf became a good and noble king in his place.

XXXII

Beowulf's first act as king was to take vengeance on the Swedes who had killed Hygelac's son. During his rule, he proved that he could overcome many perilous situations - until the dragon came.

Ready for his final battle, Beowulf goes with eleven other lords to seek the dragon. He had heard about the goblet that was stolen and finds the man who took it. Reluctant, the man leads Beowulf and his men to the cave where the dragon dwells every day. Although Beowulf is gloomy at his impending doom, he gives a speech to his men. He recounts his childhood, and how king Hrethel raised him along with his other three sons, one of which was Hygelac. One of Hrethel's sons was killed on accident by another, and this grieved Hrethel greatly. However, he could not take vengeance for his son's death without hurting his other son.

XXXIII

The king Hrethel's grief at losing his son was almost more than he could bear. He left his sons land and wealth when he passed away, and after his death there was a time of struggle between Sweden and Geatland. Beowulf fought in the front lines of the battle, and he preferred it that way. He ends his speech to the men by coming back to the dragon, declaring that he will engage in one more battle if the dragon will meet him outside the lair on open ground. He calls his warriors near and bids them farewell, explaining that he would rather not fight with sword and shield but that because the dragon is so powerful he needs a weapon to make the fight an equal match. He tells the men to wait farther away because the fight is his alone.

At the end of the speech everyone stands and goes to their respective places. Beowulf finds an arch of stone that has access to the cavern within. He cannot go down without risking being burned alive, and so he makes a war cry loud enough that the dragon can't help but hear it. The smoke and poison of the dragon's breath begins to come out of the cave, and Beowulf raises his shield and sword in preparation for the fight. When the dragon emerges, he and Beowulf regard each other warily. They are each afraid of the other, but the fight begins.

Beowulf's great shield does not protect him from the dragon's fire for as long as he would have wanted, and Beowulf lifts his arm and swings the sword, which does not pierce the dragon's flesh. Even though it was the best sword and shield in the land, Beowulf's protection failed him. Fire engulfs Beowulf, and his fellow comrades flee towards the woods. Only one remains, a noble kinsman of Beowulf.

XXXIV

The one warrior who remained behind was named Wiglaf, son of Weohstan. As he watched Beowulf struggle against the dragon's flames, he remembered all the good the Beowulf had done for him over the years. He drew his old sword, an heirloom from Eanmund, and faced the dragon. He called out to the other warriors, reminding them of their promise to Beowulf made before the battle. In the hall, Beowulf chose them because they were strong warriors and, although he wanted to slay the dragon for himself, he needs them to help. Wiglaf finishes his heroic speech by saying that he would rather die trying to help Beowulf than return with their noble king slaughtered.

With this, Wiglaf goes through the dragon's flames to help Beowulf. He calls out to Beowulf, giving him courage and reminding him of the glory and strength of his youth. The dragon's flames burn almost all of Wiglaf's armour away, but he manages to get behind the great iron shield with Beowulf. After hearing Wiglaf's bold speech, Beowulf once again has hope that he can defeat the dragon and save his kingdom. He strikes his sword at the dragon with all his strength and the sword shatters. The dragon strikes at Beowulf and gets him in the neck, and blood begins to spurt out of the wound.

XXXV

Seeing Beowulf hurt, Wiglaf reaches out even though his hand is badly burned and stabs the beast until its fire is lessened. Finally Beowulf is able to draw a knife and stab the dragon in another spot. Between the two of them, the dragon breathes its last breathe.

Slaying the dragon is Beowulf's last great feat, as he knows that the dragon's poison flowing through his blood will kill him. Beowulf walks to the edge of the arch and speaks to Wiglaf. He wants his kinsman to go down into the cavern and look at all the jewels and treasure. Beowulf reminisces about the fifty years that he was king of the Geats, and wishes that he had been blessed with a male hair to pass down his weapons and armour to. Despite the lack of an heir, Beowulf ruled with fairness and bravery. Beowulf wants to behold the treasure left behind by the dragon before he dies.

XXXVI

Wiglaf goes swiftly into the cavern to do as Beowulf wished. He sees mountains of gold and jewels, and treasures spanning many eras. He finds a banner woven with gold and picks it up. It gleams so bright that he is able to see everything. He grabs an armful of treasure and runs back up to the archway.

When he gets back to Beowulf, the elderly hero is greatly weakened by the lack of blood. Wiglaf, hoping to revive him, splashes Beowulf with water. Beowulf opens his eyes and sees the sample of treasure that Wiglaf has brought with him from the dragon's lair. He is thankful that he could live to see such treasure, and is grateful that he can leave such a gift for his people. He says he has paid for the treasure with his life, and tells Wiglaf that when he dies he wants to be buried on the headland. His burial will be called Beowulf's Barrow in honor of his memory.

Before Beowulf dies, he takes off his gold jewellery and armour, giving it to the brave young Wiglaf. He says his words of farewell, and his soul leaves his body to join his ancestors.

XXXVII

Wiglaf watches Beowulf as he dies, although it is very hard for him to do. He is sad that the hero is dead, but is thankful that the dragon who killed him is slain as well. With this last victory, he is able to say that Beowulf killed all of his enemies in battle. Beowulf paid for the treasure in the caverns with his death.

The other warriors who had hidden in the trees come out once they see that the dragon is dead. It is obvious from their walk that they're ashamed at their actions. They see Wiglaf splashing Beowulf with water, trying to wake him again to no avail. Death comes for every man, and Beowulf was not an exception.

Finally Wiglaf realizes that Beowulf is dead for good, and turns to the other warriors. Angrily, he accuses them of being cowards and not helping their king when they were needed. He says that the treasures Beowulf gave to them were wasted. He alone was able to help Beowulf, although he only succeeded in weakening the dragon by stabbing it long enough to allow Beowulf to land the killing blow. Wiglaf tells the men that the kingdom will know of their cowardice, and that they will not get any of the treasure left behind by the dragon. He says that it is better for a warrior to be dead than to live a life of shame.

XXXVIII

Wiglaf has the others announce the death of Beowulf to those who are anxiously waiting for news of the battle. The messenger goes around, telling the people that Beowulf's dead body lays beside the dragon that he slew and that Wiglaf is by his side, grieving. With their leader dead, the Geats believe that war is imminent, because historically after a great leader dies there is an upheaval with the surrounding countries trying to take advantage of the weakened state.

The messenger reminds the people of the story of Hygelac's fall. The messenger also says that he is sure the Swedes will attack them because of their long history of violence against one another. In times past, the Geats kidnaped Ongentheow's wife and the ruler of Sweden retaliated with war. Both sides fought at Ravenswood, and when hope seemed lost Hygelac came to rescue the Geats.

XXXIX

The battle between the Swedes and the Geats turned with Hygelac's arrival, and the leader of the Swedes, Ongentheow, realized that he was overpowered. Hygelac was a mighty warrior, and went after Ongentheow with his sword. A man named Wulf eventually smashed Ongentheow's head with his weapon, killing him. Ongentheow's brother took his sword and armour before fleeing back to Sweden. As a reward for killing the leader of the Swedes, Wulf was given riches, lands, and Hygelac's daughter in marriage.

The messenger finishes his story with a prediction that since Beowulf is dead the Swedes will want revenge for the death of Ongentheow. During Beowulf's reign they dared not attack, but Beowulf is no longer able to protect the Geats from the old blood feuds. The messenger urges everyone to go to where Beowulf's body lays next to the dragon, and get ready for his funeral. He also says that they should burn all the treasure that Beowulf won by fighting the dragon along with him.

At hearing these messages, the warriors become sad. They go to the cliff and find Beowulf's body stretched out beside the dragon. The great monster was enormous, at least fifty feet long where it lay dead. When they try to go into the cavern, however, they discover that the great mound of treasure cannot be touched by any human unless God allows it.

XL

The treasure in the cavern was placed under a spell so that no one who was greedy could touch it or enter the inner lair. Beowulf, however, had not wanted the treasure for himself but for his people. Wiglaf speaks, saying that the treasure belongs to the Geats, but that because of the sad way in which it was won it will be impossible to enjoy. He tells the people present how he fetched a sample of the treasure from below for Beowulf to see while he was still alive, and relates that he wanted to be buried in a burrow.

Wiglaf takes warriors down into the cavern to look at the great collection of treasure while others are busy collecting wood to make a pyre for Beowulf's body. He chooses seven men to go with him to the caverns, and they light their way with a torch. The treasure lying on the ground is easily picked up and there is so much of it that the men don't have to fight over what they want. Once out of the cavern, they push the dragon's body into the water and it is swallowed by the waves. After this is done, Beowulf is taken to Hrones-Ness to be buried.

XLI

The people of Geats make a huge funeral pyre and covered it with all sorts of armour and weapons, just as Beowulf wanted. They hold the funeral on top of a hill, and watch as Beowulf and his weapons burn. An old woman, grieving, dreads the days to come saying that they will be full of death and battle.

On the place where Beowulf's body burned, the people make a great mound. It takes them ten days, and they make sure that it is filled with all sorts of treasure. All this was done to mourn the passing of the greatest hero and beloved king that Geatland had ever known.

30255746R00214